Letters of love and sorrow

from Mothers and Fathers

to their children

lost to abortion

collected by edith m. gutierrez

On the Cover

Mary, the Mother of Jesus, raising one hand in a gesture of blessing, eyes closed in prayer, holds ~ with love ~ another woman's baby.

I chose this image for the cover because it reminds me of where Christianity began ~ in the arms of Mary ~ where hope resides, forever.

Many women and men find comfort in the thought that their children, lost to abortion, may also be held in the loving arms of the blessed Mother of Jesus.

"All generations will call me blessed."

~ Luke 1:48:

May you find peace in the promise of eternity as you read the letters of love shared on the pages of this book.

edith m. gutierrez

Dedicated to

The Holy Innocents

*"Before I formed you in the womb I knew you,
and before you were born I consecrated you."*
JEREMIAH 1:5

*"For you formed my inward parts;
you knitted me together in my mother's womb.
I praise you, for I am fearfully and wonderfully made.
Wonderful are your works; my soul knows it very well."*
PSALM 139: 13-14

For God so loved the world

that He gave His one and only Son

that who ever believes in Him

shall not perish, but have eternal life.

~ JOHN 3:16

Table of Contents

Acknowledgements

Jill Walls

God blessed Jill, a former Rachel's Vineyard retreatant, with the desire to gather the letters written by the mothers and fathers to their children lost to abortion. The title of the book was to be called: "Letters to Heaven". My heart was touched to the core with this possibility, so after a year or so passed, I asked her if I could go forth with this venture. She graciously said "yes". All of the glory goes to God!

Imogene Salvo Flynn ~ graciously translated into English the letters written in Polish.

Rudy Gutierrez ~ took the photographs and inspired new ideas for the content of the book.

Sheri Gutierrez ~ Helped with editing.

Hanna P. ~ Helped with editing.

J. L. (Jo) Hardesty ~ With love for the babies, designed the Cover and the Interior, Edited pieces other than the letters, and Prepared the book for print.

The Women and Men who shared their Letters

Thanks most of all to each of the women and men who said "yes" to this project and willingly submitted their letters to be compiled into a book. Many have said it brought further healing to them to be reminded of their spiritual relationship with their children in Heaven.

Glossary of terms

Terminology used in the letters may refer to expressions or materials that are a part of the weekend experience. Some of these might not be fully understandable to the reader. When anything is unclear, we ask that you simply read and accept the message without knowing exactly what the writer is referring to.

To help with this small challenge, we offer below a few specific terms mentioned in the content of some of the letters.

Living Scriptural exercises/spiritual exercises~
These terms are interchangeable
They are specific readings taken from the bible and created into a meditation, then re-enacted by the retreatants.

Rocks or stones ~
These are used for demonstration purposes to make tangible the hard places in their hearts that need healing.

Flowers in the meadow ~
This is a spiritual exercise on a Rachel's Vineyard weekend where retreatants are invited to visualize their children in a meadow with Jesus. At the end of this exercise, the mothers and fathers are given flowers from their child. Some people have been blessed with seeing, in their minds eye, the presence of their children in the meadow.

Spiritual relationship ~
Just as we think about and maybe even talk with our loved ones who have gone to their death before us, we invite the retreatants to do so with their children who have gone before them.

FOREWORD

On a cold February evening in Denver Colorado, eight women and two men gathered in a hotel conference room to experience a Rachel's Vineyard Post-Abortion Healing Retreat Weekend. All ten were suffering the after-effects of having been involved with an abortion. They were all on their way toward reconciliation with God and their lost children. Some were just beginning the journey; others had been seeking hope or relief for many years. But no matter how far they had come in their personal tribulations, the Rachel's Vineyard Retreat that they were about to experience would help each contrite individual come to grips with the decision that was made to abort their child.

When a participant comes to a Rachel's Vineyard weekend, he or she many feel alone and isolated, like the only misguided person who has ever made such a bad decision. Most are afraid that their self-inflicted wounds can never be healed. Some have tried to suppress their feelings ~ even to deny ~ the abortion, pretending it did not affect them. Still others arrive, fully admitting the abortion and their sorrow, but unable to see how they could possibly ever be forgiven.

Through the weekend retreat process, participants learn that, not only can they be forgiven, but that God forgives and forgets the moment one asks Him to. Further, everyone finds out that they must forgive themselves, even as they are accepting forgiveness from God. All who participate come to understand that receiving God's mercy does not mean that what they did was okay. It was a bad decision that cannot be undone. But the retreat experience teaches that it is possible to learn from the mistake, and to go on.

FOREWORD

During the retreat, participants also learn that the child God created is never really lost. Every baby existed, and still exists, in heaven. And one day, in God's time, parents and their children will be reunited.

The greatest comfort of all for the parents has to be the knowledge that the child they thought was lost is not gone forever, but rather lives in heaven with Jesus, where they will meet one day and live together forever.

Another wonderful revelation is that, although the child was only here for a short time, she or he has had an effect on the world. This baby affected the parent's own life, and therefore the lives of everyone they meet. Mothers and fathers also come to realize that, because of the decision they made, they are able to be more understanding and compassionate of the decisions faced by others. Many of these individuals become great advocates for mercy because of the forgiveness that they have experienced.

At the end of every Rachel's Vineyard Retreat, we have a Memorial Service, providing the participants with the opportunity to give recognition and honor to their children. This memorial observation includes an opportunity for parents to write letters to their children, expressing their sorrow and regret for the abortion, and the joy they look forward to when they are reunited in heaven. In this book, we share some of those profound and poignant love letters. May God bless you as you read on.

Fr. Larry Sanders, CSsR
June 2015

INTRODUCTION

Who is this book written for?

This book is for those who have had an abortion and those who have not. It is for anyone who wants to experience compassionate insight about consequences of the abortion experience and the healing process.

Many books have been written about the testimonies of women and men who have had an abortion. This book shares with readers the sorrow parents expressed to their children who were not given a chance to experience life on earth.

Why did I say 'Yes" when God called me to create this book?

Working in this ministry can be difficult and draining. It is also immensely rewarding. However, on an occasion of weariness, I asked God "how long must I work in this ministry?" God graciously revealed to me an image of all of the children I have been instrumental in spiritually re-uniting with their mothers and fathers. In that vision those dear little ones come running to greet me when I depart from this life. In the Gospel of Matthew (11:28), Jesus says: "Come unto me all you who are weary and I will refresh you." I was refreshed and pursued this new direction of outreach for post abortion healing.

What do I hope people will gain from reading this book?

• For the person who has had an abortion ~ an invitation to forgiveness, hope and healing.

• For the person who has not had an abortion ~ A means of gaining deeper insight and compassion for someone who has had an abortion experience.

INTRODUCTION

I have taken on the task of compiling these letters to provide readers with a perspective that shows that people who have had an abortion are not bad people, they are not evil people. Rather, they are people who found themselves caught up in a situation where fear set in and they accepted the lie that their life would go on as usual after their abortion. Later they found it to be otherwise.

This is a book of compassion. Those who have not had an abortion will receive insights into the heart and mind of a woman or man who has faced this tragedy, owned it, and allowed God to heal and expand their heart and soul because of it. It is a powerful witness of Christ's mercy and healing love. Those who have had an abortion, but have not sought healing will have a chance to experience, through others, some element of healing as they read the letters written by post- abortive men and women to their children.

For the past nineteen years I have had the sacred privilege of witnessing countless men and women who, in humility, offered themselves up to God to ask for healing – and received it. As a result of their forgiveness and healing, these individuals have become the most compassionate, non-judgmental pro-life witnesses I have ever met.

Many come to the retreat believing they have committed an unforgivable sin. Through the Rachel's Vineyard healing- process, these suffering souls learn that God, whose merciful love is without limit, delights in forgiving ALL sins of everyone who comes to Him and asks His forgiveness. Because theirs was an extra-long journey to self-forgiveness, these retreatants develop extreme compassion and a burning desire for others to be healed and blessed as they have been.

INTRODUCTION

Statistics on Abortion:

Statistics reported by the Alan Guttmacher Institute show that approximately 35%-45% of women will have an abortion during their reproductive lifetime.

I mention these statistics to indicate the great number of women who are in a position to experience the symptoms of post-abortion trauma; and to illustrate just how many women are suffering and feeling too ashamed to speak out.

It is important for everyone to be aware that the woman sitting next to you in the pew at church, mothers of your children's friends, ladies in the grocery store or at the park may be silently suffering because of a decision she made long ago.

This is why it is so important to be compassionate when speaking about abortion. Women who have suffered this trauma are not evil, but rather, they are women who bought the lie of abortion, and who have come to regret that decision. These women can't have a "do over." They can, however, receive forgiveness and healing through a post-abortion healing program. They need to hear compassionate words from you; words that invite them to seek out the hope and healing they long for in their wounded souls.

Edith Gutierrez
June, 2015

Information

About Rachel's Vineyard International

Rachel's Vineyard is the largest post abortion healing program in the world.

There are many retreat sites in 48 of our 50 states, as well as in 80 countries throughout the world ~ with more countries being added as we speak.

The retreat manual has been translated into many languages. The Rachel's Vineyard program format comprehensively touches the mind, the heart and the spirit. It is a Roman Catholic program designed to be suitable for all Christian faiths.

For those who want to provide this program for their own Christian church, it has been adapted to accommodate non-Catholic denominations. For more information go to www.rachelsvineyard.org. There you will find where and when retreats will be held in your state or in your country.

www.rachelsvineyard.org
1-877-HOPE-4-ME

"Healing the Pain of Abortion, One Weekend at a time"
Theresa Burke, PhD. Founder

"Neither do I condemn you."

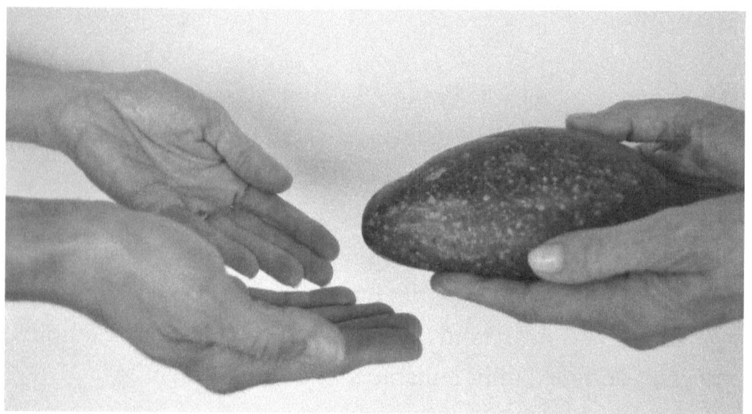

*"Let anyone among you who is without sin be the first to throw a stone at her." And once again he bent down and wrote on the ground. When they heard this, they went away, one by one, beginning with the elders; and Jesus was left alone with the woman standing before him. Jesus straightened up and said to her, "Woman, where are they? Has no one condemned you?" She said, "No one, sir." And Jesus said, "***Neither do I condemn you.*** *Go your way, and from now on do not sin again."*

~ John 8: 7-11

Setting the Stage for the Weekend Retreat

The first "Living Scriptural exercise" of the weekend is the reading from John 8:3-11. It is a reading about the woman who was caught in the act of committing adultery. She was made to stand in the middle of the town's people in full view of everybody. The people in the crowd were poised with large stones in their hands, ready to throw them at the woman for her sin. They asked Jesus what he was going to do about this, as it was the law to stone a woman caught in adultery. Jesus said that anyone among them who had never sinned should cast the first stone. Then Jesus bent down and wrote on the ground, while, one by one, each person dropped his stone and walked away. When Jesus stood up he saw that only the condemned woman remained. He asked her: "Has no one condemned you?" She replied, "No one sir". Then Jesus said: "Neither do I condemn you. Go and sin no more".

This Scriptural exercise has a profound effect on the retreatants. A stone, similar to the one in the photograph, is passed from one person to another all around the circle, in a manner, re-enacting the scene in the bible. The leader says to the person next to her: "Is there anyone here to condemn you?" The retreatant is directed to respond "No one". The leader completes the scene by saying: "Neither do I condemn you, go and don't sin anymore." That person then turns to the person seated next to her and re-enacts the same scenario. As the stone is passed around the circle, each person becomes the *sinner* and the *forgiver* ~ which sets a tone of safety because everyone in the room, including the priest, has been released from condemnation.

A brief discussion follows this exercise and the retreatants usually recognize that they have been condemning themselves for years. This initial exercise offers each person hope that they can forgive themselves in the same manner everyone in the room was forgiven.

Over the years I have witnessed the transformation of the group just with this first exercise. They immediately learn they are in a place of safety and show visible relief.

Naming the Chidren
and lifting them up to God

This is the time for parents to acknowledge their children, to name them and to lift up their lives to God.

This exercise takes place long after the retreatants have told their stories, acknowledged their pain, anger, and sorrow. At this point, they seek to honor the lives of their children lost to abortion. It is a very emotional and tender time for all.

The larger candle represents the Light of Christ in the room, the smaller candle belongs to the retreatant and is lit from the Christ candle, thereby receiving the "Light of Christ.

During this exercise, the child's candle is lit from the mother's candle, symbolizing her passing on the Light of Christ to her child. This is when the aborted child becomes real, is given a name and surrendered to the care of Jesus in Heaven.

After each child has been named and honored, there is an opportunity to sing a song to their little ones. One of the most powerful songs is:
> *This little light of mine, I'm going to let it shine.*

The names of the Children being honored in this book

Colin	Noah
Meghan	Moses
Michael	Abigail
Samantha	Gideon
Grace	Jesse
Mary	Anton
Harry	James
Angela Paul	Katie
Bartholomew	Lara
Jeremiah	Victoria Rose
Anne Catherine	Sunshine
Rajkamani Anjoli	Jamie
Samuel	Michael Joseph
Miriam	Alyssa Maria
Grace Anna	Stephen
Jeremy	Bruno
Michelle	Anna
Vincent Nathaniel	Vincent
Emily Grace	Delilah
Ann	Emily
Hayato	Eran
Job	Jo
Jasiek	Justin
Kathleen	Lauren
Rachel	Ula

THE *Letters*

If we acknowledge our sins,

God who is faithful and just,

will forgive our sins, and purify us

from everything that is wrong.

1 JOHN 1:9

PREFACE to the LETTERS

The emotions expressed in these letters range from grief and sorrow to a love and longing by the writers to meet their children in heaven.

Most women have secretly carried this spiritual and emotional burden for decades, some for as many as 50 years. Others have kept the secret locked away, even from a spouse. No matter the length of time or the situation, it is a tremendous relief when anyone is finally able to speak about their abortion, to acknowledge their child, and to bless that child with a name. All who attend a Rachel's Vineyard weekend are invited to write letters to their children, a lovely begining to the development of a spiritual relationship with their precious unborn babies.

This experience offers an opportunity to replace sorrow with joy, and to embark upon a new life.

A few of the letters in this book are written by women from other countries where English is their second language. The construction of some sentences lend a certain charm of expression so, I decided to leave them as written. Others were written in Polish and translated into English.

On the following pages, you will read in the letters, the hope these mothers and fathers have of reunion with their children in Heaven. I invite you to become a witness to the newfound spiritual relationships and the longing these parents have to merit Heaven so that they may spend eternity with the children they did not know on earth.

Edie

For terms in the letters that may not be clear, please see the Glossary on Page 11.

I am quite certain that the One who began

this good work in you will see that it is finished

when the Day of Christ Jesus comes.

Philippians 1:6

To my precious children,

When I was young, too young to get pregnant, but old enough to know better, I was foolish. I did not know the Lord as I know Him now. I let the devil play with my mind and my heart. I played in his playground of promiscuity and deserted the Lord. I have learned from those times and many others. One thing I have learned is that God is a forgiving God. He always welcomes His children back with open arms. God gave you as a gift to me and I threw you away.

I have regretted that decision ever since and pray that you will forgive me. You would have loved our life together. We would have done fun things like camping, fishing, skiing and hiking. You are in a beautiful place in the care of our Lord, Jesus Christ. I see your happy faces and know you are at peace.

Today is a new beginning for me. A beginning full of Love and wonder. For you see, I have been blessed with two beautiful children. Two children who look down on me from heaven, who pray for me and who love me for who I am. I ask that you watch over me as my angels and make sure I don't stray from my path to heaven. With God's blessings I will someday hold you in my arms and give you the motherly love you so justly deserve. Colin and Meghan, may the peace of the Lord be with you always. May you always feel my love as you wait for me to join you in that beautiful place called heaven.

I love you always my babies, Mom

I love the LORD,

because he has heard my voice

my pleas for mercy.

Because He inclined His ear to me,

therefore I will call on Him as long as I live.

Psalms 116 1-2

My Dearest Children,

How I neglected you and had no reverence of you as a human being, made in the image of God. I have many regrets but my most offensive regret is giving you up for selfish reasons. I am sorry I never memorialized you, I never mourned your loss. I never grieved. I never bore the pain of death. I snuffed out your life and tried to hide it. For this I am truly sorry. I ask again for your forgiveness. Even though I felt your forgiveness before this weekend, I know I must forgive myself. I am grateful that you had a hand in bringing me to this weekend.

As I lay here by my four babies, I feel a tenderness in my heart that I never got to express. You are a part of me that I will never forget. I just want to lay here and soak up this peacefulness and joy. Thanks for touching me from heaven and giving me another chance at being life-giving. Your love is making my world brighter with no more heaviness on my shoulders. Your love is giving me courage and acceptance. I am proud to call you my own just as my four living children. I am glad to have this connection and will be calling on you often. I am no longer ashamed and with your help will take on the world. I love you always.   Love, Mom

November 5, 2011

My beloved Michael,

Baby its mommy! I realize this is the first time I ever wrote to you and I apologize it's taken me this long to build up the courage to do it. Oh my little boy, my sweet child of mine – what did I do to you? How could I? What was I thinking and why did I allow this to happen?

I am so sorry…

Please forgive me…

Forgive my naiveness, ignorance, fear, selfishness and immaturity. I know what I did was not right. I deprived you from so many things…from birth, love, birthdays, holidays, school, dating, vacation, and a family, but above all from LIFE!!!

I am sorry for hiding your brief existence, for not even acknowledging you on medical forms.   Although I've seen you in my dreams, I often wonder what you would have looked like. Would you be tall & thin? Short or husky? What color of hair? Would you have colored eyes like your dad, grandpa and aunts? Would have you have fair skin like all the family or would you have shared my darker skin color? Would you be getting annoyed every time I sent you to brush & floss your teeth like your siblings do? Either way, whether tall, short, skinny or chunky, light or dark, green, blue or brown eyes … I would have loved you so very much.

Thank you for my flowers, they are beautiful. Thank you for your beautiful letter. I will always treasure it and hold it close to my heart. Also, thank you for forgiving me. I always wondered if you could hear me when I would talk to you. I have my answer now. Like you said, you'll always be a part of me. Thank you for loving and caring for me despite of what I did. Oh my precious child of mine, how I long to hold you just once…to kiss you and caress you. Oh GOD this hurts so much!!! I feel peace that you are with GOD. And, now know you are the angel at my side. I will continue to talk, sing and pray with you. Oh my little boy how much I miss you and love you!

Your grandma and Aunt Sandra are here, baby. I was originally going to do this on my own, but I decided not to continue depriving you any longer. They would have loved you so very much. And since they've known what happened, you've been part of their lives.

Thank you for caring and protecting yours sisters and brother. Although Priscilla knows about you I haven't gone through the details with her. But I promise I will not hide or deprive you anymore. Once the twins get older and understand I will talk to them about their older brother Michael who is in heaven and is watching over us every day. Baby, Dylan is doing so good. He is growing. It's amazing that he is 5 months old now. I know that you and GOD are watching him and protecting him all the time. I'll give him a big kiss from his Uncle Mike.

This month would have been your 25th birthday. Wow! You would have been a fine young man. I am ashamed to admit that this is the first time I acknowledge your birth month. My baby…my little boy…my dear son…please forgive this selfish mother of yours. I will take this opportunity and from this moment on, I will always remember and honor your birth month.

Happy Birthday to you…
Happy Birthday to you…
Happy Birthday my dear son…
Happy Birthday to you.
Happy Birthday Michael – I love you my dear son.

Thank you for forgiving me. Now I know I'll never feel alone again. Last night was one that I'll never, ever forget. I finally realize that neither you nor GOD hate me and that I was forgiven long ago. Sorry it took me this long to realize it and for wasting my energy elsewhere. I have a best friend now. And, we will always be a part of each other. And the day that GOD decides to bring me home, I will run up to you and pick you up, hold you in my arms and give you a big great hug & kiss and we will never leave each other again. Until then, I will long and yearn to hold you and kiss you but I rest assured that you are in a good, safe and better place with GOD. Thank you for your unconditional love. I dearly miss you. I LOVE YOU MY SON WITH ALL MY HEART AND SOUL!!!! I will not say good-bye but see you soon my love. TE AMO MIJO!!

Love always, Mom

January 25, 2015
(More from Michael's mom)

Since I lived my retreat in 2011 I knew this was the ministry where I belonged. A ministry where I can certainly make a difference share the abundant blessings and immense healing I have received. I have served in 4 retreats and in each and every one of them I learn something new, I have 'aha moments' and experience new realizations. My faith and gratitude to our merciful LORD grows as well.

I encourage team and retreatants to honor and talk to their babies at every moment and take the opportunity to acknowledge them just like their other children. This will keep their memory alive and our promise to love them from that moment on. I also share with them that we should feel honored and special that we have our own personal intercessors in heaven and our babies will be greeting us at heaven's gates. This alone should be the motivation and inspiration we need to be better individuals so we can see our babies one day.

When I got back from living my retreat I shared my experience with my kids. I actually didn't wait any longer. Michael's presence was so vivid and I had to share that with his siblings. Despite all my fears of being rejected by them I told them everything. They cried as hard as I did, but they listened attentively. At the end they hugged, kissed and assured me that they did not judge me. Michael would be part of our lives from that moment on.

Like I mentioned in my letter, the month I lived my retreat would have been my baby's birth month. I designated November 28th as Michael's birthday. There were a lot of things that are tied to this date. So starting on November 28th, 2011 and moving forward we light up a candle on a cupcake and my children, my mother and I sing Michael happy birthday. It's a beautiful but painful experience. The reality of what transpired hits me so hard.

I have also shared my story with my own siblings, nieces and nephews. Everyone in my immediate family knows about Michael including my daughter's boyfriend. We honor him by lighting a candle during a special event such as holidays, birthdays, family gatherings, etc.

My kids also talk to Michael all the time and ask him to help them through challenges and trials, to accompany them when they feel lonely, fear and/or sad. They also share with him their accomplishments. He is part of their daily lives.

Rachel's Vineyard gave me the courage and strength to acknowledge, forgive, and accept what I had done. It also gave me a wealth of peace and healing. I found GOD's and my baby's unconditional love.

Thank you for this wonderful opportunity to continue honoring our children.

> *GOD Bless you,*
> *Michael's Mom*

The LORD is near to the brokenhearted

He Helps those whose spirit is crushed

PSALM 34:18

Blessed be the God and Father

of our Lord Jesus Christ!

According to His great mercy,

He has caused us to be born again

to a living hope through the resurrection

of Jesus Christ from the dead.

1 PETER 1:3

My Darling Samantha,

You are such a gorgeous child. You have your mommy's hair, your daddy's eyes and a beautiful smile that reminds me of your grandmothers. I love you Samantha, and I really hope that you know that. It's not that I didn't want you, because I did, but mommy made a mistake and realized it after it was too late. I used to cry tears of sadness when I thought about you and missed you, and in the future I know that sadness will creep back into my heart at times, but now when I think of you standing in God's presence with that smile, I smile as well. I will always miss you my baby, but knowing that you're safe and in a good place makes it a little easier. You will always have a place in my heart and you will always be the oldest of all my children to come. When I have more children, as the oldest protect them as best you can. Let them feel your presence at times and let them know you love them. Let your daddy know too. He's been sad for a long time sweetie and he needs to know that you are safe and happy. Daddy and I love you so much. I hope that you will always know that. I will meet you again someday and that day will be the most joyous day of my life. But until that day, keep smiling and keep laughing. You are in a good, safe and happy place. I will see you soon my darling. I love you.

With all my love,
Your Mommy

Finally, fill your minds with

everything that is true,

everything that is noble,

everything that is good and pure,

everything that we love and honor,

and everything that can be thought

virtuous or worthy of praise.

Then the God of peace will be with you.

Philippians 4:8

My letter to my aborted children from Rachel's Vineyard Retreat in 2014 at the Pastoral Center, OKC, OK

Sunday, Our Lord's Day
May 25, 2014

> *Before I formed you in the womb, I knew you.*
> ~ JEREMIAH 1:5

Dearest children, Grace, Mary and Harry,

I am your mother. I felt you in my body, I felt you in my heart and I felt you in my soul.

The choices I made to terminate your lives were based on fear. Fear that I was unable to provide the basics of care: a home, clothing, even nourishment.

I believed you went back to God. I knew you'd be loved and that Our Blessed Mother would love you, watch over you, and protect you.

I am your mother, who loved you, and has loved you, all the days of my life.

Love, Mom

Dear Angela Paul,

It was good to spend time with you and remind myself what a blessing you are to me and to our family.

Thank you for your intercession last week when I was struggling with how to say "no" to team-teaching. Jesus was about your age when Mary and Joseph thought they lost Him in the temple.

Today I'm "losing" you again, to free you to do Our Father's work. Give Jesus, Grandma, Jo and Eran hugs for me and keep praying for your parents and siblings.

Love,

Mom

Dear Eran and Jo,

Both of you were more than a year old before I even knew you existed! Your parents' grief was apparent to all of us, but we didn't understand because we didn't know about you.

Jo, your daddy's grief has lasted almost thirty years. Pray with me that he can face the hard truths of his life and feel God's embrace and forgiveness.

Eran, you are grace in your mother's life. She has made better choices and is actively seeking help. Pray with me that she will allow the Sacrament of Reconciliation to help her know and feel God's absolution and tender love for her.

Although I grieve not knowing you on earth, I look forward to meeting you and living with you in heaven. Please pray with me for all our family members and for all the people we hope to help through Rachel's Vineyard.

> *Love always,*
> *Grandma*

Dear Bartholomew!

Dear Jeremiah!

(English is her second language)

You're my only children until the end of my life. You were here with me for 7 weeks. Today you would be 26 and 24, the same age I was when your lives started.

I'm your mum. I'm almost 50 now. I'm writing to ask you for something impossible - to forgive me for discarding your precious bodies - the only chance you had to step down and live fully on this earth.

Out of fear of relationships I decided to hire a paid killer, an abortionist, to destroy your bodies and forget about your souls. At that time I had no idea children could love just because I hated my parents and was never confronted about it.

It was the coldest night of my life when I decided to end your lives and afterwards I spent the rest of my life until now frightened to meet you after my death and feared I would end up in hell, maybe envying you martyrs in heaven through bloodshed and I'm the ultimate looser. Now I know that you'd have been just right for me and God would shower us with love if only I had taken the risk of martyrdom myself.

Seeing this in the bright light of the mystery of your lives, tears came down for you this weekend. You were way too young to become martyrs. I want to feel the abandonment and loneliness you must have felt when I was loving idols and not you. I want to come to you in tears because there's no other way to ask for your forgiveness.

Thanks to the healing power of Jesus this weekend I have experienced that I'm not alone, that you are alive and compassionate.

Now that you're asking me to be your mother through the barrier of death I can say: 'Let's meet at heaven's gate when the time comes'. I'm going to use any opportunity to meet you where I am in feeling for you and fighting the good fight so life won't be underestimated anywhere I go.

Your mum

Vienna, Austria May 2011

My dear children

Thank you children for your short lives. Without you my life would be really poverty stricken. I wouldn't know the truth, the way, the life.

I wouldn't know the truth because I have been raised without it. You're giving me a hint that the truth is appreciation of life no matter how impoverished or short.

I wouldn't know the way. I'd probably be dead from partying and abuse now. The way you're showing me is the way of the cross on which I can rest because it's the only free way.

(See part two of this letter on the next page ~ 45.)

Dear children,

I told Jesus that I feel sick and an outcast and asked Him what I could do to change it. When I went back to my chair you children said exactly the same thing to me that you've been outcasts and you asked me what I could do to change it.

I didn't know what to say but now I'm ready to give you an answer:
All I could do is to ask for your help:
if I said to you "I'm alone with my feelings" contradict it
if I told you "I have nothing to share with you" challenge it
if I said "I can do everything myself" question it
if I told you "we have different views of the world"
remind me that there is only one spirit.

Let me know you're happy, give me a sign, because I'm longing to get to know you. I wanna have an open account with you children. Sometimes I feel I wanna be a road sign warning travelers that they can't travel both roads; kill and be free.

Sometimes I wanna invite anyone who stops to look at my life to travel the road that wants some wear.
Had I chosen it, that would have made all the difference.
You children are my hope to get to know the way, the truth and life, no matter the pain.

Your mum

To My Dear Baby Anne Catherine,

As I write this letter, I am feeling more at peace than I have in nearly ten years. I take comfort in knowing that you are in the loving care of Our Lord Jesus. You are also in the company of two of your Grandpa's one of your Grandma's and various Aunts and Uncles, etc. If you were here with me today, you would be nearly nine years old. You would know that you have a loving father, mother, three wonderful sisters, one of your Grandma's and a niece and nephew. I am so sorry that I denied both you and all of them the opportunity to know each other. Through the healing process of the Rachael's Vineyard Retreat, I now have faith that we all will be together again one day. Until then, please know that you are in my heart and not a day goes by that I don't think of you.

Love, your Mom

P.S. I will be forever grateful for the gift of healing I received through attending a Rachel's Vineyard Retreat. As a result of this healing and reconciling the sin of my abortion with God, I returned to my Catholic faith. I am very involved in various parish ministries and so grateful to be back! I pray for the continued success of this beautiful ministry and for all the men and women who participate, that they too will realize Our Lord's unfailing love and mercy.

May our Lord Jesus Christ Himself,

and God our Father who has given us His love

and, through His grace,

such inexhaustible

comfort and such sure hope,

comfort you and strengthen you

in everything good that you do or say.

2 Thessalonians 2:16-17

Dear Ann,

I was so happy to see you this evening. I bet you were wondering when I would show up. Jesus, I'm sure, reassured you that your Daddy would come to hug and kiss you and that he could see that you were in good hands. You know I love you so much and after seeing the love in your heart, I will strive to love your living brothers and sisters, nieces and nephews all the more.

And Ann, I'm so sorry that because I was not strong enough that I deprived you of life. You are so beautiful and your brothers and sisters would have accepted you as their precious little sis. It will be such a joy when we all meet in the years that follow. Oh, by the way, as I was walking up the path I noticed you playing and dancing with Jesus. Your Mother loved to dance and some of our closest times have been in each other's arms on the dance floor. Yes, I know you already knew that. Better go now, we will bring you along and hold you up in our hour of adoration.

I love you so much, Daddy

I have told you this so that My own joy

may be in you and your joy be complete.

Today is one of your younger brothers Birthday. Even though I haven't had the pleasure to spoil you, I Love you, I can't wait until the time I will be able to meet you (If that is what God has planned for me.). I feel that your mother has forgiven herself for the choice she made or was forced into. All I can say is: "Thank you God!" and "Thank you to Rachel Vineyard's." God Bless everyone that is involved.

Your Grandmother

Dear Daughter, Rajkamani Anjoli (which in Hindi means "Princess of Offering of Both Hands"),

"….Many children came to see Jesus, and the Apostles said to them, "Don't come". But Jesus said. "Let the children come to me. I love them."

Neither can they die anymore, for they are equal unto the Angels and are the Children of God, being the Children of the Resurrection." ….Luke 20:36

"…When I became water, I looked like a Mirage;
  When I became the sea, I looked like froth and foam;
    When I became aware, the entire world became forgetful;
  When I became awake, I saw I had been asleep…"
    Poem from Sufi Poetry

My Beautiful Baby Girl,
Rachel's Vineyard woke me from a very long, deep sleep. And it was upon waking that I could finally hold you in my arms, cry for you, love you and mourn for you.

You have such a beautiful face, upturned nose, rosy cheeks, big brown eyes…..And as I tucked you into bed with me last night, I could finally begin to be the mother to you that I always longed to be all those many years ago.

For a long time, I didn't know that a big piece of my heart was missing---you were that piece---and even though it was to be for just a short time, my heart felt like it lasted for a lifetime! And now, today, Jesus will be the one holding you within His Divine and Merciful Heart until the day I will hold you again forever in Eternity.

Until then, I will be loving you with every breath that I take, with every beat of my heart, and with every song that I sing; I will hear you within the sounds of every child's laughter, in every bird that sings, in every rustling of the wind through the tall, shimmering trees, and in every ocean wave that breaks along the shoreline; I will be seeing you in every sunrise, every mountain peak, in every cloud that sails through the blue skies, and in all the stars that shine----for in the stars, I know that your light will be among the brightest of the stars---those special stars anointed by name, shining down upon my path as I ever make my way back home to you!!

I love you, In Christ's Love and Divine Mercy Forever,
Mom

In God alone there is rest for my soul,

from Him comes my safety;

with Him alone for my rock, my safety,

my fortress, I can never fall.

Hello my babies,
I want you both to know how much I love you. I know that you have been with me, watching me, trying to comfort me when I have been missing you so much. I'm sorry that I let them hurt you. I'm sorry that I wasn't strong enough to make the right choice for you guys, for me; for us. I think of you both often. This letter is very difficult for me to write. It feels like I'm being asked to say goodbye, but because of everyone here this weekend I know you're always with me.

I know that I'm not alone. I put you on my pillow last night and Jess got me a wash cloth---the perfect little blanket. He has been so helpful and comforting this weekend, everyone has. I am truly thankful and blessed to have been here. I so desperately needed this. You know, when I went to the meadow yesterday and got to hold you for the first time... I was in awe. I really do believe I went to another place, I was there, with you both and it comforts me to know that you have the other children to play with. I was so happy to see you that I kept telling myself to dream of the meadow, but I didn't.

I am still hopeful that I will see you again and until then I know God is with you---and me. I know how self-destructive I have been and I don't want to disappoint you. I know this is an ongoing journey and that scares me a little but at least I now have some courage and hope. I am smart. Sometimes I think back and I'm not sure how I ever became convinced that abortion was the answer. Maybe I was never truly convinced, but let fear guide me. Please know that I am trying. Help me heal. And know that I never left you either.

I love you forever,
Mommy

Do not let your hearts be troubled.

Trust in God; trust also in me.

In my Father's house are many rooms;

if it were not so, I would have told you.

I am going there to prepare a place for you.

And if I go and prepare a place for you,

I will come back and take you to be with me

that you also may be where I am.

You know the way to the place where I am going.

Dearest Son,

I have named you Samuel because though I did not hear or listen to God after you were conceived...God heard your cries for help. I have a hard time imagining you but in the little that I can imagine I know you are good and sweet and strong. I also know our Lord must be showing and teaching you all that I wish I could have if I had had the courage and humility to submit myself properly. I am so sorry Samuel. The Lord would have found a way for us but I was terribly prideful and blinded by my fear at the time. I would have loved you entirely. I thought I would have made a poor mother but I now know that to be a terrible lie. Would you please make a list of the things you would like to share with me later? I will do the same. And when we meet someday in heaven we can compare the two lists to see where to begin. For now rest in God's care. I give you to God now completely as Samuel's mother once did.

I will always love you and miss you terribly,
Mother

May the God of peace make you perfect and holy;

and may you be kept safe and blameless,

spirit, soul and body,

for the coming of our Lord Jesus Christ.

God has called you and He will not fail you.

1 Thessalonians 5:23

To My Dear Sweet Baby

So much sadness and heartache fill my heart when I look back at our story. How do I put into words how deeply sorry I am for what I did? There is no way to describe the incredible shame and remorse that I carried in my heart for so long. I was young and naïve when you entered my life and you were tiny and helpless. All you needed from me was love and time. But sadly, I was blind and selfish. Instead of seeing your innocence and beauty, I saw a problem. And all I wanted to do was make that horrible problem go away. So, I did and within moments you were gone. Oh my dear sweet baby, if I had only known the truth. If I had only known you were there. How could I have been so blind? Why didn't anyone tell me? Why wasn't your life one of the few that was spared? Only God knows the answers to those questions.

*No longer are you that secret
that I keep hidden from the world.
Rather, you are a
light that shines
in my heart.*

Well my sweet one, it has been more than 25 years since that horrible day. And in this time, I have grown in faith, understanding and have healed many wounds. It has been a very long journey and has come only after many years of great suffering. No longer are you that secret that I keep hidden from the world. Rather, you are a light that shines in my heart. You give me courage and reason to stand up and tell the truth. In fact, most recently, I shared your story with your two brothers and little sister. Together we pray for you and feel blessed knowing that you watch over us from heaven. I can see in their eyes the love that they feel for you.

There is so much more I could share with you, but it is time that I close. But before we part ways, I would like to share with you a special moment. You see as part of my healing journey, God led me to the Catholic Church six years ago. I had just spent time with Jesus in my very first confession and I had told Him about what I had done to you. It was the hardest moment of my entire life.

But, after 25 years of grief and pain, our Dear Lord Jesus forgave me. My heart was instantly filled with incredible relief, joy and awe. I left the church in tears at such mercy that had been shown to me. Then, as I was driving home thinking of this gift, I heard the song on the radio called ~

I CAN ONLY IMAGINE.

I can only imagine
what it will be like when I walk by your side.

I can only imagine
what my eyes will see, when your face is before me.

I can only imagine. I can only imagine.

Those words touched my heart and I realized at that moment that His forgiveness had transformed me. I was starting a new journey – a life lived in hope. And my hope was not only of seeing the beautiful face of Jesus who had shown me such forgiveness, but seeing your sweet face as well! One day you and I will walk together in God's amazing glory. I CAN ONLY IMAGINE!

Until we meet in heaven my sweet child, know that I love you with all my heart.

In Christ's Love,
Your Mom

And we know that in all things God works

for the good of those who love Him,

who have been called according to His purpose.

Romans 8:28

Dear Miriam,

This weekend I am attending a Rachel's Vineyard Retreat. There are 10 women and 2 men taking part in this time of healing. All of us have in some way experienced the sadness of taking part in the death of our unborn babies. Through the love of our Lord Jesus, each of us has been forgiven and redeemed --------- however much guilt, shame and suffering have taken place.

My message to you tonight is that I love you so very much. It has been 62 years since you were taken from me and I have thought of you each day. Your grandparents arranged for this to happen, I am sad to report, but I have forgiven them and I hope you will also. They did what they thought the best thing at the time. They never would have imagined the consequences to come in the years ahead --------- especially relative to my mental health.

*My message to you tonight is that
I love you so very much. It has been 62 years since you
were taken from me and I have thought of you each
day. Your grandparents arranged for
this to happen I am sad to report, but
I have forgiven them and
I hope you will also.*

Please forgive me, dear daughter, I am so sorry for my part in your being denied life here on earth. It was the worst thing I have ever done and I regret it. I have suffered deep remorse and shed many tears.

Through my walk with and deep love for my Lord and Savior, Jesus Christ, I know I have been forgiven. I have the assurance that you are living in heaven and loved mightily by Sweet Jesus. For this I am so thankful.

My dear husband has come to love you very much through our 55 years of marriage. We both know in our minds and hearts that you are a part of our family. Whenever we consider "our children", you are included as our child. You have a brother 9 years younger than you and a sister 11 years younger. You would love them very much and they would return the love also. When we all get to heaven it will be a glorious time as we all become acquainted. We will get to spend eternity together ------ 10,000 years and then forever more!.

Your biological father is no longer a part of my life. I pray that he and his parents have received the healing touch of Jesus. Perhaps they are a part of your life now also. He was a good man and surely would have been a good father if things had turned out differently after you were conceived.

I don't know how much you are aware of what goes on down here, but you would be pleased to know how we are working to defend the right to life for other babies and all men and women from conception to the natural end of life. This is our way to honor you.

It is our prayer that all mankind be spared the pain of abortion, genocide, euthanasia and all that comes under this heading. As we partner with our Father, Son and Holy Spirit and the community of believers, may God bless and restore the human race to His plan.

I don't know exactly God's plan for our future when we get to heaven, but I am sure of one thing: It will be far more wonderful than anything we could EVER imagine in our finite minds.

See you soon, dear child.
Your loving parents

I carried this notebook around since the retreat in my purse. When I moved into this house I put it away for safekeeping. When I opened it the other day the notes from the retreat along with a note a girl friend gave me when she knew I was making the retreat were inside the notebook. Reading my letter along with those kind words brought me back to how I felt on that Sunday. I needed to see those words and feel that feeling at exactly that moment.

I will always be amazed

    by the very Grace of God . . .

To my dearest Grace Anna,
I am so sorry this letter has taken so long to arrive to you. You have been in my thoughts your entire life. I just never had enough courage to verbalize or reach out to you until this weekend. And for that I am ever so grateful we can now begin our spiritual life together.

You were named Grace Anna:

#1. Because you had the grace to wait patiently for me until I was ready to walk through life with grace.

#2. You had a great, great Anna whom I adored and Anna never had children. So I thought it very appropriate that you be her namesake. So, now as we begin our journey, I want to read a poem that has always been a favorite of mine and now I have you to say it to.

My Grace Anna, I carry your heart with me (I carry it in my heart). I am never without it. (Anywhere I go, you go my dear; and whatever good is done by only me, is your doing, my darling). I fear no fate (for you are my fate my sweet). I have no world (for beautiful, you are my world, my true). And it's you that whatever a moon has always meant and whatever the sun will always sing is you. Here is the deepest secret nobody knows. Here is the root of the root and the bud of the bud and the sky of the sky of a tree called life; which grows higher than the soul can hope or the mind can hide). And this is the wonder that is keeping the stars apart. I carry you in my heart.

Grace Anna, I am thrilled and blessed to spend time with you now and for always.

> So much love,
> Your Mom

What marvels indeed God did for us,

and how overjoyed we were! . . .

Those who went sowing in tears,

now sing as they reap . . .

They went away, went away weeping,

carrying the seed;

they come back, come back singing,

carrying their sheaves.

Psalm 125:3-6

Written on July 20, 1999 at the end of an 8 week Post-Abortion sharing group

Dearest Jeremy

I have written this letter many times in my head over the last several weeks, but now that I sit here, the words are not coming. I started this letter once this morning but the real world of phones and problems kept creeping into my live - - - I guess that is what happened 33 years ago when I carried you in the silence of my womb. I did not realize you were there. I was so busy paying attention to my world, my problems, that I never knew you or thought of you. I am sorry for that. I have so many regrets about you. I wish I could have known you were there - - - I wish I would have listened to God trying to let me know about you. For so many years I didn't realize what happened - - - I didn't see you hidden behind the act of abortion. I didn't give you a face and name. I didn't give you life. I am so very sorry for this. You were a precious gift from God and I rejected you. It wasn't, or shouldn't have been, my choice to let you live or die. Please forgive me for taking away your life, your chance to grow, to explore, to learn, to love and to serve. I have watched your two sisters grow and become their own individual person. I realize that they were not mine to keep but to nurture and teach until they were ready to live fully the life God gave them. I never gave you that opportunity, and I am so sorry.

Over the years I have come to know Jesus. I have searched, grown, doubted and learned many things. I have loved and have been rejected; but I have always, way down deep inside, known that God loves me - - - -this truth was buried very, very deep that I dare not go there. So many times in my life I believed you were there, but I didn't see or hear you because I have never felt worth of love. I want to listen now. I want us to get to know each other. I know through my journey of faith that I truly believe in heaven; and I hold to my belief that God holds you in His arms. I can take comfort in knowing that our wonderful Father has made a beautiful place for you. I don't know what God might have had in store for you on earth, but I do know that you must be joyful in His presence now. Jeremy, your name came to me one day - - - Jesus and Mary, son and mother. Jeremy flows from the love of mother and son. I do love you. We missed so much together - - - we missed the gift of mother and child and I will never be able to recapture that. Regrets, yes, many - - -what would your life have been like. We missed a lot — there were so many times in my life I could have talked with you, prayed with you, asked for your guidance - - - most of all I asked you for forgiveness.

I know you are with my dad and my mother-in-law. I feel their presence in my life. I want to feel yours. I hope it is not too late for us. I feel at peace now. I know you are at peace and I am blessed in my life by have you watch over me. Is it okay to feel this way? It's a foreign feeling being wrapped in the arms of a forgiving God and a forgiving child. Thank you Jesus. Thank you Jeremy.

I love you. Until we meet someday, I will always picture you as my fair haired, blue-eyed son.

Love, Mom

P.S. Give a big hug to my dad, Larry and my mother-in-law - - - they were great people and great huggers.

More to Jeremy from his Mom

May 31, 2003 –

2nd Letter *to Jeremy on Rachel's Vineyard Weekend*

Dearest Jeremy

It was so good to hold you tonight. I have wanted a hug for so long and it felt so good. I haven't written you for a while, but you are still in my thoughts and close to my heart. I have felt you close by me many times, especially when I am making decisions – and you know that I don't make decisions easily. Having you as my little angel, someone who is always watching out for me, has been a blessing. When I ponder the forgiveness I have received from you and from "Our Father", I am in awe. How can I be so loved….it is beyond what I have known.

As I hold you now, hold your sprit close to me, I can feel your warmth, your love – the love I missed – the hugs I missed. But I am not sad, I actually feel peaceful and blessed by your touch. I am trying to let go of so much in my life. I know you have been there the whole time. Your prayers were felt as I worked through the pain and the forgiveness for my mom and dad.

I believe you have been there through the confusion, anger, fear and now peace. You probably know me better than any child knows their mother. You have been there to wipe my tears away – you have whispered encouragement to me when I was filled with fear – you have been faithful in your love for me. I thank you Jeremy for your blessings.

Thank you for your protection. I have heard that a son is very protective of his mother, and I do feel that. I love you, little one. I know someday I will be able to tell you that face to face – to caress your face and run my fingers through your hair – feel your kiss on my cheek – That will be heaven!! In the meantime, please know that my love for you grows daily, know that my tears are of joy that you are with "Our Father" in Heaven and that you are safe and at peace.

I told your sisters about you. They are trying to understand what happened. One of your sisters is very intuitive and she says that she knew that there was something missing in her life. They would have loved you being their older brother.
I thank you again for your unconditional love and the forgiveness that I feel. I miss you, but I hold your spirit close to mine.

My love, prayers and hugs go to you. A big thank you for the flowers you gave me tonight. It was so good to see you in the meadow. This is a beautiful Mother's Day gift!!

I love you more than those words tell you,   Mom

Yahweh is kind and merciful,

Our God is tenderhearted;

Yahweh defends the simple,

He saved me when I was brought to my knees.

Return to your resting place, my soul,

Yahweh has treated you kindly.

He has rescued my eyes from tears

and my feet from stumbling.

I will walk in Yahweh's presence

in the land of the living.

Psalm 116:5-9

To my dearest babies MICHELLE, VINCENT NATHANIEL AND EMILY GRACE....

I gave you these names as directed by the Holy Spirit.
Michelle is a sweet, soft name I envision you as a slender young woman now with curly dark hair. Strong in character, yet firm in your conviction as most Israelis are. You are a lawyer and a good one at that!!

Vincent Nathaniel is a name I was considering for your little brother. And Nathaniel is your cousin's name. Your Tio . . . . has a grandson named Nathaniel as well. You are now about 21 years old. Your Palestinian roots bring you to battle with your older sister. But our blood joins us to forget the anger that the Middle East is famous for.

Emily Grace is the name abuelita wanted for your little sister Tori. You are my flower. You are the beautiful blue eyed baby I always wanted. I'm so sorry I was selfish. I'm so sorry!!!
My babies, I'm so glad we were able to spend the quiet night together. I played Hawaiian music for you and we listened to Audry Assad. We sat in the rocking chair and I held you in my arms, one by one. I'm so glad I got to hold you in my arms and feel your love. I kissed your faces and asked you to please forgive me. This is a pain I will carry with me till the day I die and join you in heaven.

I often wonder what if, and how would our lives have turned out. …

Tonight we all slept together, all in my arms.
I cried an armful.
I'm so sorry…
Sorry I wasn't there for your first Christmas
To bathe you
To take you on vacations
To dinner
For your first Holy Communion
To wipe your tears away
To mend your torn jeans
To iron your school uniform
To buy you new shoes
To teach you to brush your teeth
To ride a bike
To take you and your friends to the beach
To choose a school backpack
To help you pick up toys and put them away
To read you a book
To put sunscreen on at the beach
To soothe a diaper rash
And to potty train you
To warm your baby bottles

Now the process I'm going through will take courage, but knowing you're with me, I'll always count on your prayers. Your prayers for your little sister, now 16, and little brother who turns 14 this week. Thank you, my children who brought me here to begin the healing process. I think you knew all along I wanted this!!! I'm so sorry it had to be this way, but I'm so grateful to be here.

I will count on your blessings and daily prayers from above. I will ask you to help guide us, all of us, to heaven to be together, and I look forward to spend eternity with you.

This weekend I heard something that brought comfort to me, "ETERNAL NOW" – What it means to me is that you are in heaven and never will experience the hardships we do on earth. Instead, you're with God and all the Angels in eternal joy. In my heart, you we're too beautiful for this world. My Angels are in heaven!!!

Michelle, 25, Vincent Nathaniel 21 and Emily Grace 20 – I love you and need you. Please be a part of my life. I accept your forgiveness and promise to move forward from here. Thank you Michelle, thank you Vincent Nathaniel, thank you Emily Grace. I love you, I love you, I love you!!!!

Love always,
Mom

PS. Each night when I look up to the stars, I look for Orion's Belt, there I see the three stars lined up…and I smile!!!!

I can see you happy and safe with Jesus and your tiny friends whose wonderful mothers I got to know during this weekend. Hayato, I can hear your laughter and giggles with these little rascals.

> . . . please pray for me to become a good disciple of Jesus who can stand firm and defend life, especially a fragile one like yours.

The Letter to Hayato,

Here I am ....your mommy....my little one!

First, I need to apologize to you that it took me such a long time to figure out how to communicate with you and you must have missed me a lot. With the help of the caring people at Rachel's Vineyard, I could finally name you, Hayato. This is the Japanese word for hawk, a big eagle-like bird, and it is also taken from the first name of our heroic Japanese ancestor " Hayato Shimoda", a land-lord who, during a time of famine, sacrificed his life to save the lives of his villagers in the 16th century. I am honored to give this name to you, knowing that you have also sacrificed your life for others, including me.

Hayato . . . my sweet boy . . . please forgive me that I could not bring you into this world as my first born son. I believe that God made a woman's body for nurturing life, not for destroying it. Your precious life should have been welcomed with joy and excitement, instead of being dealt with as a problem to be solved by others. There is no way to justify what happened. We, human-beings, have no right to decide whether you should stay or go. Please forgive my ignorance and weakness of not being able to protect you. I deserve to be stoned to death because of what I have done to you. I carried a heavy burden of guilt, sorrow, anger and inability to forgive myself for almost a half of my life. Even though I was a bad mother, I love you. Hayato ~ my darling

During the Rachel's Vineyard Retreat, I could hear your whispers from the heaven. I was able to give you a very special name and Father Larry used holy water and gave a blessing to you—a blessing in recognition of your beautiful spirit in heaven. Finally I can see you happy and safe with Jesus and your tiny friends whose wonderful mothers I got to know during this weekend. Hayato, I can hear your laughter and giggles with these little rascals.

My heavy burden was lifted at last and now I am in great peace with God. So don't worry about me. I am no longer a frantic mother who was looking for her missing child. I found you at Home with our heavenly Father, so I won't worry about you anymore. We are still separated physically but He united us spiritually. I can see your big smiles and you can see mine.

Hayato, I am looking forward to embracing you and kissing you when I am called to Home by our loving Lord. Until then, please pray for me to become a good disciple of Jesus who can stand firm and defend life, especially a fragile one like yours. I will pray for you too . . . my brave boy, to be a little more patient in waiting for me. I will be with you as soon as my work is done on earth. I think that Jesus will let you know when . . . right?

To my son, Hayato

From your mommy

If we acknowledge our sins,

God who is faithful and just,

will forgive our sins,

and purify us from

everything that is wrong.

1 John 1:9

My Dearest Kids, Job, Noah, Moses, Abigail and Gideon,

Our Sovereign Lord meant for you to receive the wonderful gift of life. As I write, I am aware that a simple or even an elaborate apology, as well as thought out as it could be or even as heartfelt as I could muster, could almost be taken as a form of mocking or minimizing what I did. I denied you that gift, the gift of life. I destroyed your chances of experiencing life on this planet.

I realize now the enormity of my actions. I realize now the blessing that you were. I realize now what my actions were really saying. It was a lie that you were just a mass of tissue or an inconvenience, someone that could just fill my days with work, a burden. I know the truth now, you were a gift, a blessing, a joy, a precious life, something to be cherished not destroyed. I know now I had no right to take that from you.

I realize now that I sacrificed you to the god of self. The enemy of our soul took great pleasure in receiving these sacrifices. I realize now as well that every moment I choose to keep silent about your existence, the memory of you, I am again sacrificing you to one of our many gods: pride, arrogance, secrecy, lies and again our favorite god - self.

Today I claim to be free of any power the enemy has had over me or any one affected by my decision of taking away your chance at life. Today I choose to honor you, the person you could have been, the blessing you could have been. Today I choose our Lord's truth.

I choose to live in the truth of His grace, in His forgiveness, in His power. He tells me, He forgives me, He loves me and He loves all my children and that is why He tells me to remember.

Although I receive a blessing from this memorial; a chance to maybe in a way mend my enormous errors, yet I realize nothing I do or say can really do that. It is true there is joy in obeying our sweet Lord in honoring you, His kids. Here I have a chance to tell a few that you, my kids really existed. You were real human beings, with as much right as any of us to have a chance at life and have a chance to choose Him. I want you to know I am doing this because it is right, it is necessary, it is what any human may desire if they were not allowed a chance at life; to at least be honored, to be remembered, to be acknowledged. I am also doing this because it would please our Savior, to own what I did, the enormity of it. To allow others in the blessing of honoring the lives He willed, the lives He purposed since the beginning of time.

I am humbled and awed in that as broken and as wretched as I am He gave me the greatest blessing. He allowed me the assurance that one day I will see you, my sweet kids, one day I will hold you. Humanly speaking no one deserves this kind of forgiveness or this kind of redemption, especially me! But I know my Redeemer and because He lives in me, I will hold you in my arms one day. I look forward to looking into your faces one wonderful day. Today I can claim with my whole heart, "what was meant for evil, God intended it all for good"
~ Genesis 50:20.

Your Mother

He heals the brokenhearted
and binds up their wounds.

PSALM 147: 3

Without the opportunity to be a retreatant at Rachel's Vineyard I would not have been able to find peace and healing. My life has been forever changed. From the start until the end of the retreat wonderful and miraculous things happened. Friendships, forgiveness, the healing presence of the Holy Spirit and knowing we were all surrounded by Jesus and His unending love.

Page 84

Dear Jesse:

If I knew then, when I was 20 years old, what I know and feel now, I would not be here today attending a Rachel's Vineyard retreat. There would be no way I would have aborted you. At the time you were conceived, you were intangible to me. Not really a baby growing inside of me. Not this precious human being created by your father and me through the Grace of God. You were something, a situation that needed to be dealt with. So without deep thought, much conversation or reflection of what we were doing or how it would affect the rest of my life, we ended your life.

Until I married your father and had children did I realize what I had done. Unforgiveable. To feel that life inside me, moving and growing, you never got that chance. I have never felt I was truly a good person or mother. How could I have aborted you and gone on to be blessed with four other children? I pushed those thoughts back deep in my mind. But they never went away.

So 37 years later I am at Rachel's Vineyard retreat trying to reconcile my decision and seek forgiveness from Jesus and you. I know you are with Jesus, in His loving arms, but you should be here with me and feel my love for you.

Until I meet with you in heaven, know how much I love you and want to be near you.
Mom

God, create a clean heart in me,

put into me a new and constant spirit . . .

Be my Savior again, renew my joy,

keep my spirit steady and willing.

My Sweet Baby Boy, Anton,

My firstborn. I'm so sorry that I deprived you of your birthright. You are the big brother of two younger sisters. You are the baby that started my journey as a mother. I knew you existed from the moment of conception, and I have never stopped thinking of you in all the years that have passed since then. I've cried many tears for you, Anton. I've longed to hold you in my arms and fill that emptiness that can only be filled by reuniting with you.

I love you, Anton. You're forever in my heart, forever a part of me.

I look forward to the day when we are together with Jesus, and I can give you a big hug and a kiss and see your smile.

  Love and prayers,
  Your Mom
  March 2013 retreat

*And the peace of God,
which is so much greater
than we can understand,
will guard your hearts
and your thoughts,
in Christ Jesus.*
PHILIPPIANS 4:7

Dearest Babies of Mine,

James, you were the first and were my most locked away hurt of record. Over forty years of denial that either of us "suffered!" My sweet boy, you are so beautiful your brown curls, honey colored skin and bright eyes with smile so huge. I swing you around and you jump in my arms! I waited SOOO LONG! Can you forgive me son? I love you with all my heart and soul!

Katie-Oh Katie, I only now have learned your name, and had my first look at you, and your curls that wind tight around your sweet face. Katie I did love your father and if he had been free to be with me at the time-I would have told him about you. I would have shared you. Can you forgive me sweetheart? Daddy found out later and was crushed. It turned out we both loved you!!

Lara-Sweet Lara my last abortion that I have the least memory of-yet God has gifted me with your beautiful name and sweet face. You have hair of soft blond darling that wisps with the wind among the flowers. I watch you crawling along side your brothers and sister. Please know that I love you no less than all of my babies. Please forgive Mama for her thoughtless and cowardly action that took away your very being. I don't even remember who your father was and I ask for your forgiveness in my selfishness!! I love you!

Charlie- You were planned and when I lost (miscarried) you, I thought maybe I was being punished-One back for taking three! Dear God! Not that! I realized that wasn't so and that you (Charlie) were not ready to come (here). It was better for you to stay with Jesus. The hard part was that I seemed to be the only one who mourned you!

Now my dearest babies I am free of guilt…and free to mourn the four of you! Free to FORGIVE MYSELF, FREE TO FORGIVE Nana for basically convincing me to get an abortion. Free to testify about my abortions, and what it has done to you and me!

While growing up-I always wanted a LARGE FAMILY. HELLO!! I HAVE ONE!

Eight Children
*James, Alyssa, Katie, Michael, Charlie,
Kara, Lara, & Amanda*

I love you!
Mama

*Surely goodness
and mercy shall follow me
all the days of my life:
and I will dwell in
the house of the
LORD forever.*
PSALM 23:6

March, 2007

My sweet little Victoria Rose;

It has been a hard, long road to this day....the day that I finally honor you and fully release you into the loving arms of God. For the last 29 years I ran away from the thought of you, the pain of not knowing you and the deep guilt and shame of my choice in aborting you. This despair blanketed every moment since that cold February day in 1978. Today all that has changed.

First of all, and most importantly, I ask you for your forgiveness for not allowing you to live; for not fighting harder for you. God had a plan for your life and I was too young, too selfish and too foolish to realize this. Please forgive me my precious only daughter.

The years have been lonely...lonely because of the loss of you, and for what my decision did to my relationship with God. I shut Him out. I shut down. I lived in darkness.

Page 90

Seeing you so clearly last night - joyfully playing with Jesus and so very happy, happier than anything could have made you here on earth, has given me the sense of peace that was missing for all of these years. I SAW the radiant joy on your face as you called out to me...what a gift! Someday, sweet one, we will hold each other close and share in the wonder of God's kingdom. We will share in a joy not comprehended here on Earth. Please dear God, let this be so.

So often I would think of the things that I deprived you by my selfish choice- your first baby steps, playing tag with your brothers amidst the fireflies in the dusk of summer nights, the excitement of Christmas morning and the joy of your wedding day. At these times, the sense of guilt, loss and regret was so strong. But from here on out, I realize that the sorrow was all mine. You enjoy so much more right where you are.

Little Victoria, I ask you to please watch over your three brothers, and pray for them. Whisper in their ears the words of truth and light. Please intercede for your family; I am sure Jesus cannot refuse anything from such a sweet little face as yours!

Thank you for your forgiveness; thank you for your love. Until we are together again, dear one, I will meet you in the Eucharist.

I love you;
Mommy

This letter is from a retreatant in Poland. Shared here in the writer's native language, it is translated on the two pages that follow.

Witam - chetnie podzielę się z panią treścia listu, który napisałam podczas rekolekcji do mojego dzieciątk

Sloneczko

moje najdroŻsze!

Tak krótko było mi dane cieszyć się tobą. Szybko przyszły wątpliwości. Czy mam zgotować ci taki los jak mój? Pozwolić przeżyć samotność, odrzucenie? Czy będę potrafiła cię kochać? Czy dam radę? Co powiedzą inni? Na twojego tatę nie mogłam liczyć. Zamknęłam więc przed tobą drzwi mego serca. Klucz do nich ma tylko Bóg. Pozostał ból, żal i tęsknota. Z mojej twarzy zniknł uśmiech. Tak długo już cię nie ma przy mnie. Jezus powiedzial że w domu Ojca jest mieszkań wiele. Wierzę że przygarnął ciebie, przytulił.

Page 92

A ja? Często myślę jak teraz wyglądasz? Jakie plany miał Bog względem ciebie? Może to własnie ty wypełniłabyś pustkę w moim domu?, podała szklankę herbaty, gdy po raz kolejny wracam ze szpitala?, przyprowadziła kapłana gdy nadejdzie kres ziemskiej wędrówki?, ile dobra zadziało by się dzięki tobie? Nie znam odpowiedzi na te wszystkie pytania. Twoja siostra i ja modlimy się, by dobry Bóg okazał mi swoje miłosierdzie, a w twoje serduszko wlał tyle miłości bys mogła mi wybaczyć, że nie potrafiłam cię pokochać i przyjąć, a Jemu zaufać do końca. Dziś kiedy Bóg otwiera drzwi mego serca widzę promyk nadziei. Wierzę,że gdy stanę przed Nim twarzą w twarz ty również wyjdziesz mi na spotkanie. Wspólnie będziemy wielbić Jego miłość i ogrom miłosierdzia.

Do zobaczenia po tamtej stronie życia-
Kochająca cię mama.

Ps. Masz jeszcze brata i siostrę.Już myślę jak cudownie będzie spotkac się razem w MIŁOŚCI.

Let us be confident, then,

in approaching the Throne of Grace,

that we shall have mercy from Him

and find Grace when we are in need of help.

HEBREWS 4: 16

*Greetings! I would eagerly like to share with you the
letter that I wrote to my child during our last retreat.*

MY DEAREST SUNSHINE-

*How little time I had to cherish you. Too quickly
doubts crept in. Can I subject you to such a fate as my
own? Allow you to experience loneliness and rejection?
Will I be capable of loving you? Will I be able to
survive? What will others say? I couldn't depend on
your father. I closed the doors of my heart on you.
Only God has the keys to those doors. All that remains
is pain, regret and longing. Smiles no longer appear
on my face. How long it has been since you were for
only a little while by my side. Jesus says that in His
kingdom there are many mansions. I believe that he
has welcomed you into his home. And I?*

So often I wonder what you look like now. What plans God had for you. Maybe you would have filled the emptiness in my home, would have been waiting with a glass of warm tea for me each time I come back from the hospital, would have brought the priest to our home when our earthly pilgrimage would come to its end. How much good you would have filled my life with thanks to your presence. I don't know the answers to these questions.

Your sister and I pray every day that God will be merciful towards me, and that God would fill your heart with forgiveness for the fact that I wasn't able to love you, welcome you and trust in the Lord till the end. Now, when God has opened the doors of my heart there exists a glimpse of hope. I believe that when I will be standing face to face with the Lord, you also will come to meet me. Together we shall worship his Endless Love and Unfathomable Mercy.

> -until we meet again on the other side
> Loving you always, Mom

P.S. You also have a brother and sister. I think how wonderful it will be when we all will be together in HIS LOVE.

O LORD my God,

I called to you for help

and you healed me.

PSALM 30:2

Dear James, Emily & Delilah,

I gave you your names and you became real to me.
I had blocked out your memory but now I can see.
I saw your faces for the first time last night.
Your brown eyes, your dimples, your smiles so bright.

You all looked so peaceful holding Jesus's hand.
You brought me some flowers you picked from His land.
I can see that Jesus has taken good care of you.
The thought of that makes me happy and I am no longer blue.

Jesus handed me baby Delilah to cuddle and hold.
That moment was so precious to me more precious than gold.
I now have to leave you, oh how will I cope.
Then I remember you are with Jesus and that gives me hope.

I made some mistakes that I will always regret,
but you are in good hands, so I do not fret.
So go enjoy yourself, pick flowers, run, play.
We will meet again in heaven when the Lord calls me
someday.

  Love, Mom

Blessed

are those who mourn,
for they shall be comforted.

Matthew 5:4

To our children, Michael Joseph and Alyssa Maria,

Can you feel the love and warmth we have for you laying here between us?

Can you hear our soft whispers telling you "we are so very sorry" and "we love you very much"?

Can you see the resemblance in our faces and smiles when we look into your eyes?

Can you feel our loving touch as we hold you in our arms?

Can you taste our tears upon your cheeks and kisses on your lips?

Can you smell our scent like we smell your sweet innocence?

Can you remember to keep these feelings locked in your hearts.

. . . till we meet again?

Love, Mommy and Daddy

This mom wrote a special note to each of her three children.

Dear Lauren ~

I love you more than anything in this world and I long to see you someday. I know your father loves you too. By now you are 19 years old. I've always wondered what you look like, the color of your eyes, or what your laugh sounds like. On this earth I will never be able to hold you or kiss you goodnight. I've always wanted to tell you I'm sorry and I'm deeply ashamed I took your life. You were innocent and deserved better. The only comfort that I have, my beautiful girl, is you are with God. I will speak with you often through prayer until the glorious day I get to kiss your sweet face.

Love Always,

your Mom.

Dear Jamie ~

I love you so much, I miss you every day. I deeply regret my decision, dearest son, and I wish I could have you back and never let you go. I sense you are a very strong and compassionate young boy, with a big heart. My heart is broken however, and I've been an emotional wreck without you. I felt like I disappointed the two people who loved me the most, Jesus and you. I'm really sorry I took your life away from you. In my heart I know you are with Jesus and your sister and brother. Please find it in your heart to forgive me. I can't wait until the day I can smell your hair and rejoice in your love.

Love you forever, Mom

Dear Justin ~

Someone once told me that God knows our prayers, even those we don't have the words for. I'm really counting on that. I'm making a promise to you; from now on I'm going to make the most of my life in respect of yours. I've learned life is valuable and a precious gift from God. I thought I would feel relief once they took you from me, but instead I've never felt more empty and alone in my life. There is nothing that will ever replace your spot in my heart. You are implanted on my mind and we are connected in spirit. Be with Jesus and your family until I'm able to dance with you in heaven. I think of you every day my son, pray for your forgiveness, and I love you more than words can express. Bless you.

Love Always, Your Mom

Kochane dzieci, Ulko i Jasiu!

Nie ma takich słów, łez, które mogłyby wyrazić mój żal i pustkę po Waszej stracie. Nie ma takich słów, które wyraziłyby mój wstyd, ból i poczucie winy za to, że Was zabiłam, za to w jaki sposób do tej pory żyłam. Nie ma takich słów, które wyraziłyby Miłość, którą do Was czuję, Miłość, którą mimo wszystko odwzajemniacie. Osiedliście głęboko, głęboko w moim sercu i tam już pozostaniecie aż do Naszego spotkania u Pana. Dzięki Wam wyszłam z ciemności i weszłam na nową, świadomą ścieżkę życia. Postaram się zrobić wszystko żeby tego nie stracić tak jak Was, żebyście mogli być ze mnie dumni. Tamtego dnia umarłam razem z wami, ale powoli odradzam się a Wy zawsze będziecie częścią mnie. Przytulam Was codziennie do mojego serca i z radością patrzę na Wasze niewinne roześmiane buzie. Jesteście podobni do swojej siostry Leny, którą też swoją decyzją skrzywdziłam. Mam nadzieję, że mi to wszystko wybaczyliście i czujecie jak bardzo Was kocham.

  PRZEPRASZAM.
   Wasza mama. Ania

*~ and
translated into
English*

> *To my dear children-Ula and Jasiek!*
>
> *There are no words nor tears which would come close in expressing my anguish and emptiness after I lost you both. No words come close to the shame, pain and guilt I feel for having killed you- until now I suffer this pain of regret and guilt. No words can express the LOVE I have and feel for you both. A love that in spite of what I did, I know you have for me. You both continue to live deep in my heart and will forever remain there until our next meeting with the Lord. Thanks to you both I have left my life of darkness and have started a new life with a clear path. I will try everything so as never to stray from Truth and lose my way again, as I lost you, so one day you can be proud of me. That fateful day, I died with you, but slowly I feel I am coming back to life and you will always be part of me. Each day I embrace you in my heart and look at your smiling, innocent faces. You both look like your sister who also has also been hurt by my decision. I hope you have forgiven me and know how much I love you both.*
>
>
>
> *I AM SO SORRY.*
>
> *Mom*
>
>

Page 101 

Dear Stephen, Bruno and Anna,

I am so very sorry I took your lives away. Know that I loved you the short time I carried you; I was, and still am, your mother. I miss you. I pray that one day we will meet so that we can be together with Jesus Christ, all the angels and saints in Heaven, and all your brothers and sisters. I have entrusted you these past years to Our Blessed Lady Mary, our Perfect Mother, to take care of you and I know that she has. Until we meet again, know again how sorry I am and how much I love you. Thank you for the flowers. That was very sweet.

Your mom.

Dear Daniel, my miscarried baby,

I love you so much and miss you. I remember the sadness and peace I felt when I buried you in the garden a long time ago. I get a chance now to write this letter to tell you how much I loved you then and still do. I pray that we will meet in Heaven with all your brothers and sisters one day. Thank you for the flowers.

I love you, your mom.

"I shall ask the Father,

and He will give you another Advocate

to be with you forever,

that Spirit of Truth who the world can never receive

since it neither sees nor knows Him;

but you know Him,

because He is with you, He is in you.

JOHN 14:16-18

Good night my sweet children.
Good night. Into the arms of God you rest!

Thank you for your forgiveness! Thank you for your love!
Thank you for the peace I now have knowing you are
with Jesus!

God in His infinite mercy has shown your faces to me. He has told me your strengths. Vincent…My oldest…Black wavy hair with piercing green eyes…Tall and straight. You are the protector… strong like Daniel in the lion's den. I see you running. Then you smile and wave at me while taking up your little brother's hand.

Micheal…You have sandy blond hair…stark blue eyes…with a softness in them that I cannot describe! You are firm footed and kind. You blow a kiss at me then take the hand of your brother… With your other hand you reach for Christ……..Then both together you are absorbed into the Light of Jesus' robes.

Rachel…My sweetness…With your straight, long, flowing, brown hair and doe-like soft brown eyes, and a purely contented smile…You are a friend of Jesus! You love Him only. You lay your head on His shoulder as he lullabies you.

Baby Mary…Shocks of black curly hair caress your ivory face with ocean blue eyes. You are smiling too. How content in the other arm of Jesus. In heaven your name is JOY!!

I know you are waiting for me.
I promise you now . . .
I will do my best here on earth...
To love Christ . . .
and my neighbor . . .
So when called. . .
I can come home to be you."

Continuation of "Good Night My Sweet Children

Samuel O Samuel… Wisdom is your strength…Smiling broadly you look at me with intense forest green eyes and platinum curly hair. You know I am not your mother but your Auntie. Turning your head you run to your mommy taking with one hand hers and the other Jesus' hand.

The peace of Christ surrounds each one as you laugh…play…sing…with Jesus and your heavenly Mother Mary.

Now…..I am finally free to LOVE you !
Remember you ! Embrace you!

I know you are waiting for me. I promise you now… I will do my best here on earth…To love Christ… and my neighbor… so when called… I can come home to be you… Until then sweet souls…I hold you in the chordae tendindeae of my heart and in the light of my soul…My Holy Innocents…. you shall never be forgotten again !

LOVE…LOVE…LOVE,
Your Mama

July 13, 2013

My Baby Kathleen,

I am not sure what to say to you; I ask for your understanding and forgiveness in aborting you and ending your sweet life.

Darling, you did not deserve to die and it grieves me not only for the loss of your life, but also for the horrible way in which you died.

I apologize to you and hope you can forgive me. I was frightened and confused when I went to a doctor who confirmed I was pregnant with you.

I do take full responsibility for my regretful, shameful actions. I'm disappointed that I trusted and followed this doctor's instructions, which caused your death. I didn't seek advice from anyone else, including asking your daddy for his support to keep you. But more importantly, I didn't ask God for His help and direction in doing what was best for you, His child. Please know that I love you and think of you often; look forward to the day when we meet and pray you will run into my arms. I'll hold you ever so tightly and shower you with hugs and kisses, my dear baby girl.

One day your sister and brothers will be thrilled to meet you too, as will your daddy.

I love you my sweet angel safe in God's arms.
Love you so much, Mommie

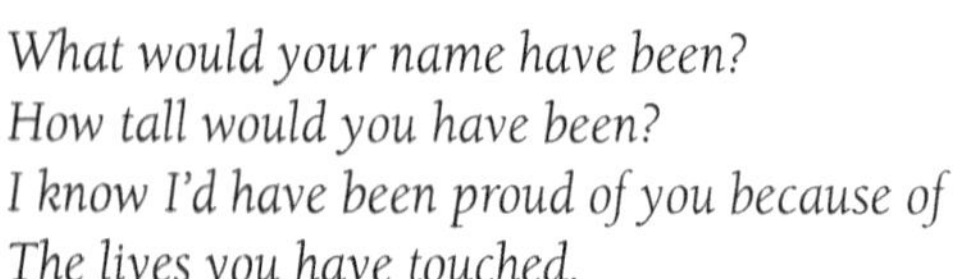

What would your name have been?
How tall would you have been?
I know I'd have been proud of you because of
The lives you have touched.

I know you stand beside me now,
You have always been right by my side.
I will someday see you in heaven and
Will no longer hide our love.

His name is John and I gave him away.
Gave him up before he was born
Because I was not brave enough to say no,
I don't want to give up my child.

Sometimes we are weak and sometimes we are strong.
Strong enough to bear the pain of regret,
But weak enough to know we were wrong.
Wrong in our decision, wrong with our pride.

Was I too scared to take the responsibility,
Or just afraid of the pain?
Frightened of the consequences,
Or guilty and ashamed.
How could I have been so selfish, so afraid to take a stand?

How could I have agreed to giving you up and taking your
life that day?
I pray each day and ask for your forgiveness,
To accept me, as I am, a fearful and weak woman, who
was afraid to take a stand?

Did I decide to give you up and make my life a little easier?
A little less complicated, or lighten my load.
Did I think you'd be a burden, a problem,
A decision I'd regret!

I did not follow my heart,
I did not follow my dreams,
I followed someone else's wishes,
And lost a son it seems.

I wait to meet this child of mine,
For I know he is in God's arms.

Will he be tall or short?
Will his smile be crocked or straight?
Has he longed for me as I have longed for him?
Each waiting breath I wait.
Wait to hold him in my arms,
Wait to kiss his cheek
Wait to tell him how much I love and miss him
And then wait to weep and laugh together.

For he has been waiting for me and I've been waiting for him.
Soon we will be together and nothing can tear us apart.

I know God will have my child standing by Him
the day I stand before Him.
My child will be smiling with open arms.
He will have forgiven me my sin
And love me for all my faults,
And our love will begin, begin, yes our love will begin!

Someday I will meet him
Someday he will raise me up
Someday I will meet him
And know that I am loved

Where are you now?
Playing in heaven and waiting for me?
Watching me on Earth
And knowing someday I'll be your Mother in heaven

I pray, each day, that you are happy,
I pray, each day, that you are loved,
I pray, each day, that God has you in His arms,
And graces you with His love.

Walk awhile with me,
For I miss you badly today.
Are you playing with your friends in heaven?
Or missing me today?

I know I will meet you,
I hope it will be soon,
To hold you in my arms
And tell you I'm sorry
That I gave you away that day.

Forgive me for my failures
Forgive me for not being strong enough
To stand up for you on that day
And saying I'd had enough.

I ask you to forgive me
I ask you to pardon my sin
You are my cherished child
And someday we will begin our life together

What have I taken from you?
A chance to fall in love,
To have a first kiss
Fall in love and marry your loved one.

I cannot give these moments back to you
I won't even try, but know you have always been in my thoughts
and prayers as each day has passed me by.

How do I give these earthly moments back to you?
Or does it really matter?
God has you in His arms,
So does nothing else really matter?

Who would you have been on this Earth?
Whose lives would you have touched?
A football star?
The homecoming queen?
The person who created world peace?
Or invented the cure for cancer?
I've taken you gift away from the world
By my selfishness
I pray you will forgive me Lord for not trusting you enough.
Enough to know that it would have worked out,
That you would have protected us and made it right.
Enough to know that you had us in your arms and all the world
would become right!

I've taken away your time on Earth
I've taken away your dreams?
I've taken God's Earthly plans for you
And all the lives you were to touch and heal!
I've taken away my chance to grow old with you and watch
you become a man or woman I'm proud to say is mine.
I've taken away your laughter, tears and smiles from my life
And all the joys we could have shared

I know someday I'll be with you,
And hold you in my arms.
We will laugh, dance and play together,
And I will stand proudly and shout that you are mine!

It is important to note that the difficulties surrounding the abortion issue can and do involve more people that just the woman who had the abortion. It involves a boyfriend, a husband, siblings, parents, grandparents, and friends. The following is information and a poem composed by a gentleman whose father performed abortions.

"Abortion has a web of sometimes unrecognized effects. This Rachel's Vineyard participate is grieving all lost children because his father performed abortions".
~ Author of the poem ~ *Flowers in the Meadow.*

Flowers in the Meadow
(The flowers all have names)

I didn't know how to grieve them

These children with no names

I didn't know how to grieve them

I couldn't see past my shame

I didn't know how to grieve them

Their numbers were too great

The man I loved caused their death

I couldn't get past my hate

But now you have given me hope

Your precious gifts I have received

For when you named your babies, then I knew…

It's your babies that I grieved

You have allowed me to a sacred place

A meadow very near

Life giving water flows from His throne

And He wipes away every tear

Here I see your children

Smile and dance and play

They even brought me flowers

They told me "we're ok"

Now I know your stories

We have shared each other's pain

Perhaps our healing can begin…

These precious flowers now all have names

Blind Child
(Composed by a former retreatant)

I met a young blind boy
At park side one day.
Feeding the birds at his feet
He did say . . .

I feel there's a sadness
Too deep in your soul.
How troubled you are.
How grief holds you so.

Whatever is wrong
Perhaps, I can help
My mom always knew
Not to doubt in yourself.

I thought to myself . . .
How could this be?
His eyes blind – pointed forward
Not even on me.

Who is this child?
How does he dare!
To know what's in my heart.
And why does he care?

Who is this boy?
With no eyes is he blessed.
How could he know
What lies deep in my chest?

He is only a blind child
Feeding some birds.
Seeds stick to his hands.
To my soul stay his words!

Abortion. Don't believe the LIE!

RACHEL'S VINEYARD
A Gift of Love and Life

We came together that Friday evening, twelve women in varying stages of pain, our hearts begging for solace, our minds holding us separate and apart. Each suffering in our own way, we looked past one another across the great chasm of sorrow that walled us off from all that might have offered comfort, sadly embracing the alienation that kept us from fully loving, from completely accepting any love that was offered.

Some of us harbored terrible anger, some another form of fear. Some of us suffered sadness so deep as to be unfathomable, and of course there were hints everywhere of denial. But the emotions that had brought us to this crossing of heretofore-parallel paths were shame and guilt—and the motive power that had driven us to this convergence was the overwhelming need of the prisoner for release.

When we met, there was no light in any of us. Our eyes were dull, our expressions empty. We stood at first, distant from one another in a sort of ragged circle, acknowledging introduction, accepting nothing. We stood like puppets with invisible strings holding us upright, our true framework too weak to be relied on. We were embarrassed and humiliated, but we were not yet humble. We were victims of a pervasive cancer of the soul, lepers afraid to touch one another for fear of final desiccation ~ or was it healing we weren't sure we could handle?

Less than 48 hours later, everything had changed for us all. Our upside down worlds had been turned right side up. Our collective darkness had been flooded with God's Light, our despair replaced with hope.

"Behold," our Lord said, "I make all things new." Each of us had heard that promise at one time or another. But none of us had believed it could apply to us, the fallen, the sinners who thought we deserved no mercy. And yet, He did this for us. He made us new, beloved daughters of His heart.

Now there is brightness in our eyes and our once drawn faces express the joy of our youth. Indeed, we are younger, softer of countenance, lighter of step. Our smiles come, now, more easily and again these smiles fill our eyes as they did once upon a long ago, before we bought and paid for the most awful of all a woman's sorrows.

And now I commend you to God,

and to the word of His grace

that has power to build you up

and to give you your inheritance

among all the sanctified
Acts 20:32

On the pages that follow,
we offer a few of the many
Retreat Evaluations
collected over the years.

Additional information,
quotes, and resources
are also included.

Evaluations from Rachel's Vineyard Retreats

After each retreat the participants are given a form and asked to provide a brief response to what was their overall impression of the retreat and what was personally most meaningful to them.
Each evaluation was written anonymously.
As I re-read the evaluations from all the years,
the most consistent words were:
WOW, AMAZING, LIFE-CHANGING!

Here are a few quotes gleaned from the evaluation forms over the years.

• *"This retreat was such a reward that I feel relieved from the huge burden which I have been carrying for many years. It was a truly life-changing experience."*

• *"Wow!   Words are inadequate for the amazing healing power of this retreat."*

• *"This retreat has opened my eyes, heart and soul up to receiving Jesus Christ into my heart. I am so grateful & thankful that I was accepted to be able to attend this retreat. It has helped me put my guilt, anger, sadness at the feet of Jesus and finally accepted his forgiveness."*

• *"Very healing. After so many years of hiding or keeping silent it was freeing to be able to have others discuss their abortions and then do more that talk – healing activities, scripture, reconciliation and adoration."*

• *"What a wonderful experience of healing and complete forgiveness. I have been on many retreats that helped me on my spiritual journey, but this has changed my life. I certainly have become closer to God, my wife, now my complete family. I also understand death in such a beautiful way. It will help in offering my love to those who share lost loved ones. I am leaving the retreat with my cup over-flowing."*
• *"It was nothing that I thought it was going to be and everything that I had secretly hoped for."*

• "Awesome. The best experience of my life. I have been on many retreats and I have never felt closer to God."

• "This retreat went way beyond my expectations. It is so evident that every part of the retreat has been birthed by the Holy Spirit. The love and appreciation I have for the team and the Catholic Church for implementing this program are beyond words."

• "A gift from God – very much needed today. Christ is truly present-offering unconditional love and forgiveness to sinners- such as me. A true blessing."

• "I feel blessed to have been a part of such a life-changing event."

• "Best Gift I could give myself."

• "I thought it was the most gentle release of letting go of all the shame, guilt, self-loathing."

• "This opportunity and its capacity for healing is a Godsend!"

• "My overall impression is one of awe. I found everything that took place to be so beautiful, so planned to the most minute, caring detail. I felt like I was in great, non-judgmental hands. I'm quite honestly overwhelmed but happy beyond my expectations. Thank you for the bottom of my heart. Before it was my awful secret, carried pretty much alone, now I see I'm not alone."

• "Heavenly – out of this world, I had no idea how beautiful this would be and what an excellent program it is."

• "A most healing and beneficial investment of time. "

• "The best retreat I've ever been on."

• "I never imagined I could be forgiven for abortion. This retreat made my baby so real to me and I was able to forgive myself and put her to rest with the Lord."

• "A most blessed and sacred time of healing. The presence of Jesus is truly visible and the Holy Spirit's healing quite miraculous. "

- *"The retreat was so much more than I expected."*

- *"Two words – Pure Excellence.*
        This retreat was a life-changing weekend."

- *"Total spiritual 'revamp'"*

- *"Very compassionate, prayerful & sacred."*

- *"It was the most inspiring experience I have been involved in."*

- *"I wish everyone who has had an abortion could attend."*

Evaluations from men

- *"Grace filled, healing time. Nothing like this that I ever attended. Very Special! I have never seen so many very courageous women. I am very humbled to know their lives, sorrows. I can never grasp the depths of hurt and pain unless I was to hear them here this weekend."*

- *"This retreat has completely changed my appreciation for what people go through as a result of abortion. I have a new understanding of what my wife has experienced and gone through all these years."*

Most meaningful Spiritual exercises

Another part of the evaluation form was for the participants to state what was most meaningful to them. These are just a few statements gleaned from their forms:

- *"I found great meaning in so much of the retreat & the exercises. The ones that stand out the greatest and most impactful: 1. The rock, 2. the water bowl with naming my child & raising her up to God, 3. Being given the doll to start to make a connection with my child, 4. The Memorial Service."*

- *"The Memorial Service gave me the final release and closure for my guilt and grief."*

• *"The idea that my children in heaven might want a relationship with me. The idea that I can have a relationship with them. That they might care about and help their living sister."*

• *"That our husbands were included in all of the activities. While not his child, he had the opportunity to spiritually adopt my child. Love that idea!"*

• *"It's hard to select any one thing, as the components flowed together and built on each other beautifully. All the experiential components were amazing. It's difficult to choose, but the exercise of the rock sticks out as powerful. The touching Jesus' cloak exercise was another thing that stands out."*

• *"The ability to make the child real, to serve the child up to God and mourn and grieve for the loss."*

• *"The Memorial Service. It was beautiful and provided so much closure and now I can love my child without the pain of the shame and guilt of the abortion."*

• *"Certificates of Life, the little angels."*

• *"Naming our children, and the memorial service where we read our letters and said "good-bye." Very hard, but very worth it."*

• *"The ability to bond with my baby. I never called him 'my baby.' Thank you for making this acceptable. I would have never done this on my own. I needed permission."*

• *"Confession and Memorial Service"*

• *"What I had lost was not real to me until I touched the soft fabric of my dolls, then the realization of my lost babies flooded me."*

• *"Making our babies real to us and the comfort and love I felt."*

Redemptive Suffering

"When human suffering is understood in its deepest meaning, it ceases to be something negative that is experienced in a passive manner. Rather, one becomes free to meet suffering with courage, seeing it as an opportunity for active and positive collaboration in the work of human redemption. Through God's grace, it can be transformed into an irreplaceable service for souls, and is no longer wasted."   ~ Jason Evert

The following testimony is an example of suffering which was transformed into service for souls.

"I know without a doubt it was God's providence that brought me to Rachel's Vineyard. It was 5 years ago and I was going through my first confession to become Catholic. I was an RCIA candidate at Light of the World. It was an amazing journey just to get to that point as I had decided to become Catholic alone, without my husband or any family members encouragement. My husband is not Christian and my family is a mix of Christian backgrounds. I just felt God's pull to the Catholic Church. I was a nervous wreck preparing for my very first confession - 40 plus years of sin including an abortion. I hadn't shared this detail with many people in my life, let alone a priest. I carried an 8 1/2 x 11 piece of paper into the confessional and blurted out "abortion" in the middle.

Father Michael of Light of the World compassionately looked at me and said that my penance was complete. I had already spent the last 15 years of my life living in guilt and shame. He then asked if I had ever heard of Rachel's Vineyard. He handed me the name and number of a woman, Lori, and suggested I give her a call. Little did I know that day, that she would become such a dear friend and spiritual guide to me in the future. It took me more than a year to make that call. Many times I went to the RV website during that year, but I never had the courage to take a step. Until one day, I just decided to do it. What did I have to lose?

I called Lori. I will never forget our conversation. I drove in circles in my car afraid that I might lose the connection. I could have talked to her for days. We must have talked for over an hour. For the first time in my life, I was speaking with someone who had experienced the same horrible tragedy. Her warmth, love and listening ear put me at ease immediately. By the end of our conversation I knew I wanted to join the weekend. However, it was going to be a challenge.

My husband isn't Catholic and didn't understand why I would want to go away for a weekend and share my story with strangers, and to top it off my three children were very, very young at the time. How could I leave them alone for three days? Could he take care of them by himself? My parents didn't know my story and neither did my friends. He couldn't go to them for help while I was gone.

Obstacle upon obstacle was placed in front of me, but somehow each was overcome with prayer and support from Lori and many other prayer warriors within the RV family.

Finally, the big day arrived and I said a tearful goodbye to my sweet babies and made the long drive to the hotel. I was so scared and had no one to talk to. I wondered how I would enter the hotel lobby? Would the people who work there know that I had had an abortion? But, those fears all went away the second I was greeted with a smile and escorted to my room by a gentle soul. The woman told me she too had an abortion and had been through the retreat as well not long before and that many people were praying for me at that very moment and that it would all be okay.

Within an hour, I met my fellow retreat friends. There were maybe 10 of us in the group and we came from so many backgrounds and our stories were all so different. But, as I looked around the room I realized we all had something in common - we were all deeply hurt and ashamed of what we had done. We could hardly look each other in the eye without turning away in shame.

Little did we know that first night, that over the next days we would slowly shed that skin and draw close to each other and even closer to God. Within a few short hours, I forgot all about the obstacles and issues of my husband and three children at home and the fact that my parents didn't have any idea what I was doing. You see, I told everyone I was just going away on a "women's spiritual retreat." In a way, this was true. You see, because I left my troubles behind, I was able to give my attention completely to the task in front of me. Without interruption, I was going to walk through the pain of my past and move forward to healing and a new beginning in life.

And, that is what Rachel's Vineyard gave to me; a transformation. Just as Jesus spent three days in the tomb and Jonah spent three days in the belly of the whale, I too spent three days in isolation from the outside world and all of its' distractions. I emerged from the weekend a new person full of light and a burning desire to speak the truth to the world.

I left RV no longer ashamed, but rather overjoyed at the thought that I wasn't alone, that I had been healed and that I had a child in heaven. I felt a light inside of me and I wanted to be a window to others to show them the light too. And now, I had a mission. I wanted to tell the world about my child and about the truth of abortion. And as soon as I asked God for direction, he paved the way.

Since my weekend, God has led me on an incredible adventure. Each day I ask him what can I do for you today, Lord? I am your hands, feet and voice. I will go wherever you need me and say whatever you want because this is no longer about me, but about you and your glory. I have this confidence and peace within me because of God, but it is also because of my experience with RV.

Here are just a few of the places where God has asked me to share my story over the last 3 years since I completed my weekend:

1. I met with Father. Alvaro at St. Mary's and became a contact for other priests and women at the church if needed.

2. I shared my story with my parents and my family

3. I shared my story with the SW Deanery of priests and offered my services to them.

4. I spoke at the March for Life in 2013

5. I stood up and spoke briefly at the Rachel's Vineyard First Annual Fundraiser

6. I shared my story with my Endow Group and then members of my group at the Catholic Biblical School

7. I was asked to speak at Mullen HS (unfortunately the engagement was cancelled an hour before my talk)

8. I spoke at Regis HS Girls Division last fall and am speaking again this spring

9. I held focus groups with HS students over the summer to learn more about their views on pro-life

10. I am researching the idea of creating an I-Phone application for teens which gives them resources, links, testimonies, and talking points related to pro-life

11. I am organizing a committee to evaluate the current sexual education curriculum and needs of the students at St. Mary's Parish School where my children attend. Children are born pro-life. We just need to help them understand why.   I didn't have that education growing up.

I continue to ask God each day to use me to make a difference and to let me be a voice. Thank you RV.

Had an Abortion?

As a Catholic priest, I have listened to the deep regret that many women carry after their abortion. Any priest will tell you that, whether in the confessional or in private discussion, women who feel the need to talk about their abortion carry tremendous pain and regret. A woman has never told me that she is proud of her abortion; on the contrary, it is one of the heaviest burdens that she carries. Hence the reason she goes to the priest: to receive God's forgiveness and healing.

Several times, as I've spoken with a woman who's had an abortion, I've thought to myself during the conversation: This woman was lied to. She didn't freely choose this. She felt pressured. She was scared. As priests we deal with the aftermath of abortion. We see what many people who promote and defend abortion don't see; the pain, guilt and sorrow that these women carry.

There is good news, however, for any woman who's had an abortion. Her regret can lead her into the loving and merciful arms of the Lord. Each time I speak with a woman who's had an abortion, particularly if it's in the context of the sacrament of reconciliation, my words are the same: no sin is greater than God's love and mercy. The Lord desires to forgive and He will forgive.

The Church is here for You.

Those in the pro-abortion movement may not be there for the woman after her abortion, but the Church is.

I want to encourage any woman who's had an abortion and is experiencing pain not to be afraid to turn to the Lord and to ask for His healing. He wants to embrace you. No sin is greater than the love He has for you. As a priest, it is a deeply moving experience when I am able to speak words of forgiveness to a woman who has had an abortion. Do not be afraid to turn to Him. And if you know someone who needs God's mercy and healing because she's had an abortion, encourage her to turn to the Lord. She needs to know that He is waiting to embrace her with His love.

~ Excerpt from an article by Fr. Michael Najim

Our Lady of Guadalupe
Patroness of Unborn Children

Virgin of Guadalupe,
Patroness of unborn children,
we implore your intercession.

Console parents who have lost the gift
of life through abortion, and lead them
to forgiveness and healing through the
Divine Mercy of your Son, Jesus, the Christ
in whose Holy Name we pray. Amen

The most recent Popes of our times have uniquely expressed great compassion for the women and men who have had an abortion experience.

On the following pages we share brief excerpts from the writings and homilies of Pope Saint John Paul the Great, Pope Benedict XVI and Pope Francis.

Pope Saint John Paul the Great

In his encyclical letter Evangelium Vitae
(THE GOSPEL OF LIFE, *paragraph 99*),
this Saint has a special message for
women who have had an abortion ~

The Gospel of Life

"I would like to say a special word to
women who have had an abortion.
The Church is aware of the many factors
which may have influenced your decision,
And she does not doubt that in many cases
it was a painful and even shattering decision.
The wound in your heart may not yet have healed.
Certainly what happened was and remains terribly wrong.
But do not give in to discouragement and do not lose hope.
Try, rather, to understand what happened and face it honestly.
If you have not already done so, give yourself over
with humility and trust to repentance.

"The Father of mercies is ready to give you His forgiveness
and His peace in the Sacrament of Reconciliation.
You will come to understand that nothing is definitively lost,
and you will also be able to ask forgiveness
from your child who is now living in the Lord.
With the friendly and expert help and advice of other people,
and as a result of your own painful experience,
you can be among the most eloquent defenders
of everyone's right to life.
Through your commitment to life,
whether by accepting the birth of other children
or by welcoming and caring for those most
in need of someone to be close to them,
you will become promoters of a new
way of looking at human life."

~ Pope Saint John Paul the Great, March 25, 1995

Pope Benedict XVI

"It is necessary that society as a whole must defend the conceived child's right to life and the true good of the woman ...

" As your work has shown, it will likewise be necessary to provide compassionate care for women who, having unfortunately already had an abortion, are now experiencing the full moral and existential tragedy of it.. Many dioceses and volunteer organizations offer psychological and spiritual support for full human recovery. The solidarity of the Christian community cannot dispense with this type of co-responsibility. (2011)

Pope Benedict XVI

Speaking to the United States Conference of Catholic Bishops, Pope Benedict XVI explained: *"God's love does not differentiate between the newly conceived infant still in his or her mother's womb and the child or young person, or the adult and the elderly person. God does not distinguish between them because he sees an impression of his own image and likeness (Gn 1:26) in each one."* (2006)

"Life is the first good received from God and is fundamental to all others; to guarantee the right to life for all and in an equal manner for all is the duty upon which the future of humanity depends." (2007)

A Wound to the Human Heart

In February of 2011, Pope Benedict XVI delivered a message to members of the Pontifical Academy for Life and other prolife leaders who were examining post abortion problems. Excerpts are included on the facing page and below.

• *"Abortion resolves nothing, rather it kills the child and destroys the woman."*

• *"The issue of postabortion syndrome — namely the severe psychological problems commonly experienced by women who have had an abortion voluntarily — reveals the irrepressible voice of moral conscience and the terrible wound it suffers each time a human action betrays the human being's innate vocation to good."*

• *"Through moral conscience God speaks to each of us, inviting us to defend human life at all times, and in this personal bond with the Creator lies the profound dignity of moral conscience and the reason for its inviolability."*

EXTRAORDINARY JUBILEE of MERCY

DEC. 8, 2015 - NOV. 20, 2016

"IT WILL BE A HOLY YEAR OF MERCY."
-POPE FRANCIS

Pope Francis

"Mercy Is the Lord's Most Powerful Message!"
"Forgiveness Is the Joy of God"

"God's mercy can make even the driest land become a garden, can restore life to dry bones (cf. Ez 37:1-14). ... Let us be renewed by God's mercy, let us be loved by Jesus, let us enable the power of his love to transform our lives too; and let us become agents of this mercy, channels through which God can water the earth, protect all creation and make justice and peace flourish". ~ Easter Urbi et Orbi message on March 31, 2013

The "Year of Mercy" will be observed by the Church starting on December 8, 2015 through the following November 20, 2016. This is a special "Jubilee Year," a kind of observance that happens basically once per generation. The theme of mercy is so important to this Pope, because it is at the heart of the Gospel and of the needs of the world today. The ministry of **Rachel's Vineyard is right at the center of that proclamation of mercy.**

On the following page, is the special prayer composed by Pope Francis for the Jubilee Year of Mercy. In this prayer, the Holy Father entreats the Lord to make the Jubilee of Mercy a year of grace so that the Church, "with renewed enthusiasm may bring good news to the poor, proclaim liberty to the captives and the oppressed, and restore sight to the blind."

Pope Francis ~ Prayer of Mercy

Lord Jesus Christ,
you have taught us to be merciful like the heavenly Father,
and have told us that whoever sees you sees Him.
Show us your face and we will be saved.
Your loving gaze freed Zacchaeus and Matthew from
being enslaved by money; the adulteress and Magdalene
from seeking happiness only in created things;
made Peter weep after his betrayal,
and assured Paradise to the repentant thief.
Let us hear, as if addressed to each one of us,
the words that you spoke to the Samaritan woman:
"If you knew the gift of God!"
You are the visible face of the invisible Father,
of the God who manifests his power above all by forgiveness
and mercy: let the Church be your visible face
in the world, its Lord risen and glorified.
You willed that your ministers would also be clothed in
weakness in order that they may feel compassion for those in
ignorance and error: let everyone who approaches them feel
sought after, loved, and forgiven by God.
Send your Spirit and consecrate every one of us with its
anointing, so that the Jubilee of Mercy may be a year of grace
from the Lord, and your Church, with renewed enthusiasm, may
bring good news to the poor, proclaim liberty to captives and the
oppressed, and restore sight to the blind.
We ask this through the intercession
of Mary, Mother of Mercy,
you who live and reign with
the Father and the Holy Spirit
for ever and ever.
Amen.

Trusting in the Mercy of God

Rachel's Vineyard is a ministry based on trusting in the mercy of God. As an outgrowth of that mercy, retreatants develop a trust in God's mercy for the children they lost through abortion. We take comfort in the passage where Jesus says "let the children come unto me." These children can be entrusted to the heavenly care of Jesus, Mary, Joseph and the saints and angels in heaven. Just as we speak in our hearts to the loved ones who have gone before us, so also we can speak to these holy innocents in our hearts.

The letters in this book from the mothers and fathers of aborted children are filled with love and sorrow. Some have claimed that because of this regretful experience, they have returned to the Church. Many have also expressed that there is the sense that these children have lead them to healing and self-forgiveness.

Rachel's Vineyard provides a safe space for mothers and fathers to mourn the loss of their children. Perhaps the most gratitude expressed on the weekend is for the Memorial Service held on Sunday. This helps bring closure for participants by providing an opportunity to honor their children and put them to rest. There is such interior joy when they unexpectedly receive a "Certificate of Life" with their child's name on it. This certificate is placed among other treasures in their lives. There is peace surrounding this moment.

Rachel's Vineyard

"Healing the Pain of Abortion,

One Weekend at a time."

Theresa Burke, PhD. Founder

Memorial for Unborn Children

Memorial for Unborn Children

As an art student, Martin Hudacek of Slovakia was moved to create a sculpture to draw attention to the devastation abortion can bring to the woman, and that through the Love and Mercy of God, reconciliation and healing are possible.

The sculpture shows a woman in great sorrow grieving her abortion. The second figure in the work is the aborted child, presented as a young child, who in a very touching, healing way, comes to the mother, to offer forgiveness.

Martin, who named the work "Memorial for Unborn Children," said the sculpture also "expresses hope which is given to believers by the One who died on the cross for us, and showed how much He cares about all of us."

"I love that the child is reaching out to touch the mother's head. I can imagine the mother sensing the touch and believe that she will stand up, taller than before. I believe that this image is very strong and touching, possibly leading to the first step of healing for the mother who has aborted her children." (Julie Thomas)

☙

Psalm 30:11-12

You have turned my mourning into dancing;

You took off my sackcloth and

clothed me with a garment of joy,

so that my soul may sing

praise to You and not be silent.

O LORD my God,

I will give thanks to You forever.

☙

On the Rachel's Vineyard Weekend Retreats
we play music with words that touch the soul.
This is one such song, written by Michael John Poirier:

Forgiven

Dear Daughter, weep no more,
the Lamb has opened Heaven's door.
Offer your secret agony with the
Mother who weeps on Calvary.

Dear daughter, persevere in the love
that brings you hear. Yes, there is a time to
grieve, and there comes a time when you
must believe. You are forgiven, you are forgiven.

Every sorrow turns to joy,
As you remember, only remember,
You are a treasure to me.

Dear Mama, weep no more,
I wait for you at Heaven's door.
Offer you secret agony with
The Mother who weeps on Calvary.

Dear Papa, persevere in the love that brings
You here. Yes, there is a time to grieve, and
There comes a time when you must believe.

You are forgiven, you are forgiven.

The year was 1964; I graduated from high school, but the understanding in our family was that girls didn't go to college, so I had to turn down a scholarship and went to work as a receptionist at a local hospital. In 1966 I married Rudy Gutierrez, my life's partner, my friend, and the father of the four daughters we raised together in Northern California.

Fast forward – Having home-taught the two younger daughters in Junior High and High School, my love for learning was rekindled. I attended community college with my daughters and received an AA degree in Liberal Arts. That felt so wonderful I went on to get a BA in Psychology. Learning there is not much one can do with a Bachelor's in Psychology, I prayed and asked God what He wanted me to do with the rest of my life. Soon thereafter, He sent me to a Conference in Los Angeles called "Human Life International" where I learned about "post abortion healing". Before attending that conference, I really had no idea what this was, but the call sat on my heart as the answer to prayer. After that profound experience, I enrolled in Santa Clara University and received a Master's Degree in Counseling Psychology in 1997.

The year prior to receiving my degree, I began working with the Respect Life Director in Oakland, CA with the program called Rachel's Vineyard Post-Abortion Healing. The work felt anointed and to this day I consider it a privilege to be part of the organization.

During the 1970's and the 1980's I participated in a number of pro-life ministries. What I noticed about myself, even then, was that when standing in front of abortion clinics, while the others were shouting to "save the babies", my own heart wept for the women who entered and came out of the clinic. I believe it was then that the Lord was preparing my heart for the work He ultimately led me to ~ the work I do continue to do now.

I am a Licensed Professional Counselor in Colorado and the love I have for women and men who have been wounded by the choice they made in the near or distant past (sometimes more than 50 years ago), leaves me with a desire to inform the public ~ especially the pro-life groups ~ of the sorrow experienced by so many people.

I want everyone to know that these are good women and men who made the terribly unfortunate choice of abortion.

I want those who have experienced an abortion to know that God loves them, forgives them and is waiting for them to come to Him and ask for forgiveness.

Then . . . *"As far as the east is from the west,*
so far hath He removed your transgressions."
Psalm 103:12.

Afterword

Let there be comfort to those who have experienced multiple abortions knowing that each occasion can be forgiven. It takes extra courage to step forward to be healed, but remember the words in Luke: *"For this reason, I tell you that her sins, her many sins, must have been forgiven her, or she would not have shown such great love. It is the person who is forgiven little who shows little love. Then he said to her, your sins are forgiven . . . your faith has saved you; go in peace."*   ~ Luke: 7: 47-50

"The Lord never tires of forgiving.
It is we who tire of asking for forgiveness."
Pope Francis - (First Angelus as Pope March 17, 2013)

Resources

Post Abortion Healing Programs

• Rachel's Vineyard International: www.rachelsvineyard.org
A Post-Abortion Retreat for women and Men

• Rachel's Vineyard of Colorado: www.rvrcolorado.org
A Post-Abortion Retreat for women and Men

• Project Rachel: www.hopeafterabortion.com

Support Systems

Women Made New: www.womenmadenew.com
Face it - Own it – Heal it / Behold, I make all things new Rev. 21:5

Catholic Therapists: www.catholictherapists.com

Endow: www.endowgroups.com

Silent no More: www.silentnomoreawareness.org

Books

FORBIDDEN GRIEF: Theresa Burke, PhD. Founder of Rachel's Vineyard
A SEASON TO HEAL: Penny Salazar & Lucci Freed
HER CHOICE TO HEAL: Sydna Massee & Joan Phillips
FORGIVEN AND SET FREE: Linda Cochrane
A POST-ABORTION BIBLE STUDY FOR WOMEN
Healing a Father's Heart: Linda Cochran and Kathy Jones
POST-ABORTION BIBLE STUDY FOR MEN
THE JERICHO PLAN: David Reardon
WAITING FOR A NAME: Cynthia Cerny

"Healing the Pain of Abortion, One Weekend at a time"
Theresa Burke, PhD. Founder

Prayer for the Culture of Life

Oh Holy Mother Mary, we pray today for all

mothers and fathers who may feel

overwhelmed by the news of their pregnancy.

Intercede for them that God may give them

the grace and the courage to say "yes" to this new life.

May they have the grace and the courage

to reject the lie of abortion as presented

by the world and the devil

and say "yes" to life.

Let us fully recognize and acknowledge that,

as wrong as it is, an abortion experience

cannot be undone; it cannot be reversed.

In this year that Pope Francis has announced to be

a Jubilee Year of Mercy, let us pray for women

and men who have an abortion in their past . . .

Let us pray that they come to know and believe

that God will forgive them for this sin

they think is too big to forgive.

We pray that they come to know that
our loving God is ready and willing to forgive
those who approach the throne of grace
in sorrow and ask forgiveness.
For those who have not had an abortion,
help us to speak compassionately about those who have.
Many have left the church because of an abortion;
help us use words that will not impede
their coming back, but rather
be welcoming of their return.

We pray also that the Culture of Life
will grow with the assistance of women and men
who have been healed from an abortion.
We pray that everyone, especially everyone
in our churches, will come to see that
because of the healing received from Jesus,
post-abortive women and men can
"become the most eloquent defenders of life"
as Pope Saint John Paul the Great stated in
"The Gospel of Life."
Amen.

Prayer by Edith Gutierrez • Permission to copy is granted.